iPod touch®
FOR
DUMMIES®

by Tony Bove

WILEY

Wiley Publishing, Inc.

iPod touch® For Dummies®

Published by
Wiley Publishing, Inc.
111 River Street
Hoboken, NJ 07030-5774
www.wiley.com

Copyright © 2009 by Wiley Publishing, Inc., Indianapolis, Indiana

Published by Wiley Publishing, Inc., Indianapolis, Indiana

Published simultaneously in Canada

About the Author

Tony Bove is crazy about iPods, iPhones, and iTunes: He not only provides free tips on his Web site (www.tonybove.com), but also took the plunge to develop an iPhone application (Tony's Tips for iPhone Users). Tony has written more than two dozen books on computing, desktop publishing, and multimedia, including *iLife '04 All-in-One Desk Reference For Dummies* (Wiley), *The GarageBand Book* (Wiley), *The Art of Desktop Publishing* (Bantam), and a series of books about Macromedia Director, Adobe Illustrator, and PageMaker. Tony also founded *Desktop Publishing/Publish* magazine and the *Inside Report on New Media* newsletter, and he wrote the weekly Macintosh column for *Computer Currents* for a decade. Tracing the personal computer revolution back to the 1960s counterculture, Tony produced a CD-ROM interactive documentary in 1996, *Haight-Ashbury in the Sixties* (featuring music from the Grateful Dead, Janis Joplin, and Jefferson Airplane). He also developed the Rockument music site, www.rockument.com, with commentary and podcasts focused on rock music history. As a founding member of the Flying Other Brothers (www.flyingotherbros.com), which toured professionally and released three commercial CDs (*52-Week High, San Francisco Sounds,* and *Estimated Charges*), Tony performed with Hall of Fame rock musicians. Tony has also worked as a director of enterprise marketing for leading-edge software companies, and as a communications director and technical publications manager.

Dedication

This book is dedicated to my sons, nieces, nephews, their cousins, and all their children . . . the iPod generation.

Author's Acknowledgments

I want to thank Jimi Eric Bove for providing technical expertise and performing valuable testing on his iPod touch, and John Paul Bove for iTunes, Windows, and iPhone expertise. I also want to thank Rich Tennant for his wonderful cartoons, and Dennis Cohen for technical expertise beyond the call of duty. And let me not forget my Wiley editors, Paul Levesque and Virginia Sanders, for ongoing assistance that made my job so much easier. A book this timely places a considerable burden on a publisher's production team, and I thank the production crew at Wiley for diligence beyond the call of reason.

I owe thanks and a happy hour or three to Carole McLendon at Waterside, my agent. And finally, I have executive editor Bob Woerner at Wiley to thank for coming up with the idea for this book and helping me to become a professional dummy — that is, a Dummies author.

Publisher's Acknowledgments

We're proud of this book; please send us your comments through our online registration form located at http://dummies.custhelp.com. For other comments, please contact our Customer Care Department within the U.S. at 877-762-2974, outside the U.S. at 317-572-3993, or fax 317-572-4002.

Some of the people who helped bring this book to market include the following:

Acquisitions, Editorial, and Media Development

Senior Project Editor: Paul Levesque

Executive Editor: Bob Woerner

Copy Editor: Virginia Sanders

Technical Editor: Dennis Cohen

Editorial Manager: Leah Cameron

Media Development Project Manager: Laura Moss-Hollister

Media Development Assistant Project Manager: Jenny Swisher

Media Development Assistant Producers: Angela Denny, Josh Frank, Shawn Patrick, and Kit Malone

Editorial Assistant: Amanda Foxworth

Sr. Editorial Assistant: Cherie Case

Cartoons: Rich Tennant (www.the5thwave.com)

Composition Services

Project Coordinator: Katherine Crocker

Layout and Graphics: Claudia Bell, Carrie A. Cesavice, Samantha K. Cherolis, Reuben W. Davis, Joyce Haughey, Christin Swinford, Ronald Terry

Proofreaders: Cynthia Fields, John Greenough

Indexer: Claudia Bourbeau

Publishing and Editorial for Technology Dummies

Richard Swadley, Vice President and Executive Group Publisher

Andy Cummings, Vice President and Publisher

Mary Bednarek, Executive Acquisitions Director

Mary C. Corder, Editorial Director

Publishing for Consumer Dummies

Diane Graves Steele, Vice President and Publisher

Composition Services

Debbie Stailey, Director of Composition Services

Contents at a Glance

Table of Contents

Introduction

This is the part in which I'm supposed to introduce the iPod touch and tell you why I wrote this book, but frankly, I'm so blown away by the iPod touch and all it can do that all *I* want to do is get you started with it.

Yes, I have a history with iPods: I wrote *iPod & iTunes For Dummies,* which I recommend for studying iTunes more closely. iTunes is the free software that controls the iPod touch from your computer. I even wrote an application for the iPhone and iPod touch, called Tony's Tips. But enough about that: Obviously I'm a true fan of the iPod line, and I think you should be too! So, on with the book!

About This Book

The publishers are wise about book matters, and they helped me design *iPod touch For Dummies* as a reference. With this book, you can easily find the information you need when you need it. I wrote it so that you can read from beginning to end to find out how to use your iPod touch from scratch. But this book is also organized so that you can dive in anywhere and begin reading the info you need to know for each task.

I didn't have enough pages to cover every detail of every function, and I intentionally left out some detail so that you won't be befuddled with techno-speak when it's not necessary. I wrote brief but comprehensive descriptions and included lots of cool tips on how to get the most out of your iPod touch.

At the time I wrote this book, I covered the most recent iPod touch model and the latest version of iTunes. Although I did my best to keep up for this print edition, Apple occasionally slips in a new model or new version of iTunes between book editions. If you've bought a new iPod touch with features not covered in the book, or if your version of iTunes looks a little different, be sure to check out the Tony's Tips section of my Web site (www. tonybove.com) for updates on the latest releases from Apple.

Conventions Used in This Book

Like any book that covers computers, mobile devices, and information technology, this book uses certain conventions:

> ✔ **Choosing from a screen or menu:** When I write "Choose Settings↪ General from the Home screen," you tap Settings on the iPod touch Home screen and then tap General on the Settings screen.

With iTunes, when I write "Choose View➪Hide Browser," it means you should click the View menu, move the cursor down to highlight the Hide Browser option, and click to select it.

✔ **Sliding, scrolling, and flicking on an iPod touch:** When you see "Slide the screen" or "Flick the screen," I mean you need to use your finger to slide the screen. When I write "scroll the list on the iPod touch Settings screen," I mean you should use your finger to slide the list so that it scrolls.

✔ **Clicking and dragging on the computer:** When you see "Drag the song over the name of the playlist," I mean you need to click the song name (in iTunes), hold the mouse button down, and then drag the song with the mouse over to the name of the playlist before lifting your finger off the mouse button.

✔ **Keyboard shortcuts on the computer:** When you see ⌘-I, press the ⌘ key on a Mac keyboard along with the appropriate shortcut key. (In this case, press I, which opens the Song Information window in iTunes.) In Windows, the same keyboard shortcut is Ctrl-I (which means press the Ctrl key along with the I key). Don't worry — I always tell you what the equivalent Windows keys are.

✔ **Step lists:** When you come across steps that you need to do in iTunes or on the iPod touch, the action is in bold, and the explanatory part follows. If you know what to do, read the action and skip the explanation. But if you need a little help along the way, check out the explanation.

✔ **Pop-up menus:** I use the term *pop-up menu* for menus on the Mac that literally pop up from dialogs and windows; in Windows, the same type of menu actually drops down and is called a drop-down menu. I use the term pop-up menu for both.

A Quick Peek Ahead

This book is organized into six parts, and each part covers a different aspect of using your iPod or iPhone and iTunes. Here's a quick preview of what you can find in each part.

Part 1: Touching All the Basics

This part gets you started with your iPod touch: powering it up, recharging its battery, using its multi-touch interface and onscreen keyboard, and connecting it to your computer. You also find out all the techniques of an iPod touch road warrior: setting your alarm and multiple clocks for time zones, keeping time with your stopwatch, changing your display settings, setting the passcode to lock up the device so others can't use it, and setting restrictions on content and the use of applications.

Part II: Filling Up Your Empty Cup

This part shows you how to download to your computer songs, albums, podcasts, audio books, movies, TV shows, and music videos from the iTunes Store, and applications from the App Store. You also find out how to buy music, podcasts, videos, and applications directly on your iPod touch. I also show you how to synchronize your iPod touch with your iTunes library on your computer, and with your personal contacts, e-mail accounts, Web bookmarks, and calendars.

Part III: Playing It Back with Interest

In this part, I show you how to locate and play all types of content on your iPod touch — music, audio books, podcasts, movies, TV shows, videos, and slideshows of your own photos. You discover how to control playback, adjust the volume and equalize the sound, and play YouTube videos.

Part IV: Touching the Online World

This part describes how to use your iPod touch and the Safari application to surf the Web. You also find out how to check and send e-mail, look at your stock portfolio, and check the weather in your city and other cities. I also show you how to display maps and driving directions.

Part V: Staying in Touch and Up-to-Date

In this part I explain how to use your iPod touch to locate and communicate with friends on Facebook, MySpace, Twitter, and other social networks and instantly chat with people. I also show you how to enter and edit calendar entries, and enter and sort contacts. You also find out how to update or restore your iPod touch, and reset its settings.

Part VI: The Part of Tens

In this book's Part of Tens chapters, I provide ten tips that can help make your iPod touch experience a completely satisfying one, and describe ten iPod touch apps that will rock your world.

Bonus Chapters

Lucky reader! You can take advantage of my previous forays into iPodland by checking out the online bonus chapters associated with my *iPod & iTunes For Dummies* book on the companion Web site at www.dummies.com/go/ipod6e. Scattered through those chapters you'll find even more great informational nuggets. Topics include:

- ✔ Choosing audio encoders and quality settings for importing music
- ✔ Preparing photo libraries, videos, address books, and calendars for your iPod touch
- ✔ Managing multiple iTunes libraries and copying your library to other hard drives or computers
- ✔ Getting wired for playback and using accessories

Icons Used in This Book

The icons in this book are important visual cues for information you need.

Remember icons highlight important things you need to keep in mind.

Technical Stuff icons highlight technical details you can skip unless you want to bring out your inner technical geek.

Tip icons highlight tips and techniques that save you time and energy — and maybe even money.

Warning icons save your butt by preventing disasters. Don't bypass a Warning without reading it. This is your only warning!

On the Web icons let you know when a topic is covered further online on a Web site. For example, I call your attention to specific areas within Apple's site (www.apple.com), and I refer to tips I provide on my site at www.tonybove.com (in the Tony's Tips section).

Part I
Touching All the Basics

The 5th Wave — By Rich Tennant

"You know, a lot of symphony orchestras are putting their music online these days as a way to reach new audience members."

1 touch all the basics in this first part to get you started with your iPod touch as quickly as possible.

I start you out with a power punch in Chapter 1: opening the box, sorting out its contents, and then powering up the iPod touch and connecting it to iTunes (the software that synchronizes content with it). You also find out how to get the most from your battery.

Next, I show you how touch it — the multi-touch interface that drives the iPod touch. You get a quick tour of the Home screen, the icons, and the onscreen keyboard, including tricks like how to quickly type numbers and switch the keyboard to another language.

Then, in Chapter 3, I set you up with the right time and date, clocks for different time zones, alarms, the timer, and the stopwatch. You discover how to set a passcode to lock your iPod touch so that no one else can use it. You also find out how to set the display's brightness, turn the sound effects on or off, change the wallpaper that appears on the locked screen, and set restrictions so that your kids can't jump onto YouTube or download explicit tunes.

Powering Up Your iPod touch

*Y*ou hold in your hands the greatest portable music player in the world, which also happens to be the greatest portable video and game player. But that's not all: With built-in wireless Internet connectivity, the iPod touch defines an entire new class of . . . thing.

I want to call it a *device,* but it's so much more — the iPod touch puts the entire world in your pocket. Not only can you download tunes and games directly to your iPod touch, but you can also select from a library of over 50,000 applications (known as *apps*) that offer everything from soup to nuts. Apps come in the form of databases that serve up local restaurants based on your location; utility programs that connect you with social networks like Facebook; and a plethora of navigation, lifestyle, health, sports, reference, finance, productivity, and travel aids. Apps even let you send and receive e-mail and visit your favorite Web sites.

Less than a third of an inch thick and weighing only 4 ounces, the iPod touch is really a computer — it uses a flash memory drive and an operating system that can run applications. It shares the design characteristics and many of the features of its more famous cousin, the iPhone, with the same built-in speaker and volume controls on the left side and the same touch-sensitive glass display. And with the iPhone 3 Software Update for the iPod touch (available seperately for older models), it can do nearly everything an iPhone can do, except make cellular-service phone calls and pinpoint its exact location with the Global Positioning System (GPS). Even so, the iPod touch can pinpoint its approximate location with Internet-based location services, and you can make phone calls using the Skype app, an Internet connection, and an external microphone. It also offers stereo Bluetooth for using wireless headphones and microphones.

So what's in the box, and what can it do?

Thinking Inside the Box

Apple excels at packaging. Don't destroy the elegant box while opening it, and check to make sure that all the correct parts came with it, as shown in Figure 1-1. Keep the box in case, heaven forbid, you need to return the iPod touch to Apple — the box ensures that you can safely return it for a new battery or replacement.

Dock Connector to USB Cable

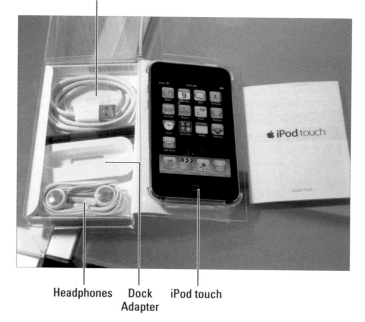

Headphones   Dock   iPod touch
Adapter

Figure 1-1: Inside the box for the iPod touch.

The iPod touch is supplied with the following:

- Stereo headphones (often called *earbuds*)
- A dock adapter fitted for Apple's Universal Dock
- A Dock Connector to USB cable

The cable connects your iPod touch (or its dock) to your computer or to the AC power adapter using a USB (Universal Serial Bus) connection — a way of attaching things to computers and bussing data around while providing power. The cable has a USB connector on one end and a flat dock connector on the other end to connect either to a dock or directly to an iPod touch.

Outside the box

There are a few things you may want to have around that are not in the box. For example, even though you don't really need an AC power adapter or dock — you can connect the iPod touch directly to your computer to recharge your battery — a power adapter or dock is useful for keeping the battery charged without having to connect the iPod touch to your computer.

The earbuds supplied with your iPod touch may not suit your tastes, but there are a hundred other headphone products that might. You can get all kinds of accessories, including headphones, speakers, the Apple Universal Dock, other docks, and AC power adapters, from the online Apple Store (www.apple.com/store), the physical Apple Store, or other stores such as Amazon.com and Frye.

Computer and software not included

You still need a computer and iTunes to manage your content and your iPod touch. These things are not in the box, obviously.

You've seen requirements before — lots of jargon about MB (megabytes), GB (gigabytes), GHz (gigahertz), and RAM (random access memory), sprinkled with names like Intel, AMD, and Mac OS X. Skip this section if you already know your iPod touch works with your computer and you already have iTunes. But if you don't know whether it will work, and you don't have iTunes yet, read on.

You need the following:

- **A PC or Mac to run iTunes:** On a PC, iTunes version 8 (version 8.2 as of this writing) requires Windows XP (with Service Pack 2), or either 32-bit or 64-bit editions of Windows Vista, running on a 1GHz Intel or AMD processor with a QuickTime-compatible audio card, and a minimum of 512MB of RAM; 1GB is required to play HD-quality videos. You need a DirectX 9.0–compatible video card with 32MB of video RAM (64MB recommended) to watch video, and a 2GHz Intel Core 2 Duo or faster processor to play HD-quality videos from the iTunes Store.

  With a Mac, iTunes version 8.2 runs on all versions of Mac OS X (Leopard and Snow Leopard), and on older Mac OS X (Tiger) versions 10.4.9 (version 10.4.10 or newer required for iPhone). You need a 500 MHz processor or better (Intel or PowerPC), and at least 512MB of RAM; 1GB of RAM is required to play HD-quality videos. You also need an Intel PowerPC G5 or a 1GHz PowerPC G4 or faster processor; 16MB of video RAM, to watch video; and a 2GHz Intel Core 2 Duo or faster processor to play HD-quality videos from the iTunes Store.

- ✔ **USB connection:** You need a USB 2.0 connection (also called a *high-powered USB*) on your computer. All current-model Macs and many PCs provide built-in USB 2.0.

  For details about using USB, visit the companion Web site for *iPod & iTunes For Dummies,* 6th Edition, at `www.dummies.com/go/ipod6e`.

- ✔ **iTunes:** Make sure you have the current version of iTunes, which also includes QuickTime for playing video. You can download iTunes for Windows or the Mac from the Apple site (`www.apple.com/itunes/download`); it's free.

Discovering What Your iPod touch Can Do

Play music, audio books, videos, and games; communicate with friends in social networks; make travel reservations and see maps of the entire world; check the weather and your finances; and keep track of all your appointments. You can do all this and much, much more by using apps and connecting to the Internet.

Whipping up a multimedia extravaganza

Portable DVD players are cute, but they don't come anywhere close to being as convenient as an iPod touch for playing video. The iPod touch is the Swiss Army Knife of media: It plays music, music videos, TV shows, movies, audio books, slideshows, and *podcasts* (audio and video episodes designed to be downloaded to your iPod touch).

The convenience of carrying content on an iPod touch is phenomenal. For example, the 32GB iPod touch can hold around 7,000 songs. That's more than a week of nonstop music played around the clock.

Apple offers the following sizes of iPod touch models as of this writing:

- ✔ **The 8GB model** holds about 1,750 songs, 10,000 photos, or about 10 hours of video.

- ✔ **The 16GB model** holds about 3,500 songs, 20,000 photos, or about 20 hours of video.

- ✔ **The 32GB model** holds about 7,000 songs, 25,000 photos, or about 40 hours of video.

All three models use the same battery that offers up to 36 hours of music playback, or 6 hours of video playback.

For a nifty chart that shows the differences between iPod models, see the Identifying iPod Models page on the Apple iPod Web site (`http://support.apple.com/kb/HT1353`).

How do you get 7,000 songs (or for that matter, any number of songs) onto your iPod touch quickly? If you have an iTunes library of songs, you can fill up your iPod touch by connecting it to your computer (as I describe later in this chapter) and synchronizing it with iTunes (as I describe in Chapter 5). You can also download songs from the iTunes Store, as I describe in Chapter 4.

Even audio books and videos — some of your favorite TV shows, plus music videos and full-length movies — are just a touch away on your iPod touch, or a click away in iTunes.

You use iTunes to organize your content, make copies, burn CDs, and play disc jockey without discs. To find out more, see my other book, *iPod & iTunes For Dummies* (Wiley Publishing, Inc.).

The iPod touch can also show pictures. Its 3.5-inch, widescreen, multi-touch display offers 480-x-320–pixel resolution at 160 dots per inch for crisp photos and video pictures. You organize your photos on your computer and then transfer them to your iPod touch using iTunes, as I describe in Chapter 9.

Communicating with the world

Your iPod touch can sense Wi-Fi networks. (Wi-Fi, short for wireless fidelity, is a popular connection method for local area networks and the Internet; you can set up your home or office with Wi-Fi using an inexpensive Wi-Fi hub, such as Apple's AirPort Extreme.) After it finds one or more networks, the iPod touch lets you choose one to connect to the Internet, and it can remember the settings for that network so that it can automatically choose the same network again.

With a Wi-Fi connection, you can use the Safari app to browse the Web and interact with Web services, and you can use the Mail app to send and receive e-mail. Stocks, Maps, and Weather are apps that show information from the Internet. You can also use the YouTube app to play YouTube videos on the Web. All these apps are supplied with your iPod touch.

You can download more apps to your iPod touch by connecting to Wi-Fi and the Internet, and tapping the App Store icon. You can download music, videos, and podcasts by tapping the iTunes icon, as I describe in Chapter 4.

You also use apps to connect to the Internet in other ways than browsing. For example, popular social networks such as Facebook and MySpace offer apps to connect you with your friends on those services. Google offers an array of services through the Google Mobile app, including the ability to edit documents and spreadsheets, use the Gmail service, and share calendars and photos. The Twitterific app lets you post tweets on Twitter, and the WhosHere and Loopt apps can connect you directly to other iPod touch and iPhone users for chatting.

Rolling the dice

Many of the apps you'll find listed at the App store are especially designed to take advantage of three distinct features of the iPod touch: its multitouch display; its accelerometer (which detects acceleration, rotation, motion gestures, and tilt); and its ability to detect its physical location.

For example, Motion X Poker — actually a dice game — uses the accelerometer to let you roll the dice by shaking the iPod touch. The Flick Fishing app senses motion so you can cast a fishing line with a flick of the wrist. And for really precise motion, try rolling a steel ball over a wooden labyrinth of holes in the free Labyrinth Lite app.

Sensing your iPod touch's location is a very useful feature. The Showtimes app uses your iPod touch's location to show the movie theaters closest to you. The Eventful app uses your location to display local events and venues, and the Lethal app can tell you the dangers which could surround you — the hostile animals, the likelihood of crimes, the prevalence of disease, and the potential accidents and disasters.

So now you know a bit about what the iPod touch can do. It's time to fire up this baby and start rockin' out.

Connecting to Power

Awaken your iPod touch by pressing the Sleep/Wake (On/Off) button, which is located on the top of the iPod touch, as shown in Figure 1-2. (The black oval on the back and near the top is the Wi-Fi antenna — don't cover this up if you're trying to access Wi-Fi.)

If you press the Sleep/Wake (On/Off) button again, it puts the iPod touch back to sleep and locks its controls to save battery power.

You can turn the iPod touch completely off by holding down the Sleep/Wake (On/Off) button for about two seconds, until you see the Slide to Power Off slider; then slide your finger across the slider to turn it off. You can then turn it back on by pressing and holding the Sleep/Wake (On/Off) button. To save battery power, you should plug the iPod touch into AC power or your computer before turning it back on from a completely off state. (For battery details, see the "Facing Charges of Battery" section in this chapter.)

Wi-Fi Antenna   Sleep/Wake (On/Off) button

Figure 1-2: The top of the iPod touch.

You can supply power to your iPod touch (and charge your battery at the same time) by using the provided cable and your computer, or you can use an optional AC power adapter that works with voltages in North America and many parts of Europe and Asia.

On the bottom of the iPod touch, you find one large connection called the Dock Connector and a smaller connection for headphones, as shown in Figure 1-3. The Dock Connector mirrors the connection on the end of a dock — your iPod touch fits snugly in a dock, and then the dock offers the Dock Connector for your computer.

Dock Connector   Headphone Connector

Figure 1-3: The bottom of the iPod touch, showing the Dock Connector.

Do you want your iPod touch to stand upright? Just connect it to an Apple or a third-party dock and then use the cable supplied with your iPod touch to connect the dock to your computer or power adapter. The dock keeps your iPod touch in an upright position while connected and also provides connections for a home stereo or headphones. Some docks offer built-in speakers. A dock can be convenient as a base station when you're not traveling with your iPod touch, because you can slip it into the dock without connecting cables. You can pick up a dock at an Apple Store, order one online, or take advantage of third-party dock offerings.

To connect your iPod touch to your computer, plug the flat connector of the supplied cable into the iPod touch Dock Connector (refer to Figure 1-3), and then plug the USB part on the other end into the USB port on your computer.

You can connect the USB end of the supplied cable to either the Apple (or third-party USB) power adapter for power, or to the computer's USB 2.0 port for power. As soon as you connect it to the computer, iTunes starts up and begins syncing the iPod touch (see Chapter 5). After syncing, the computer continues to provide power through the USB 2.0 port to the iPod touch.

Why USB 2.0? What happened to 1.0? Most PCs and all current Macs already have USB 2.0, which is all you need to provide power and to sync an iPod touch with your computer. Although you can use a low-powered USB 1.0 or 1.1 connection to sync your iPod touch, it doesn't supply enough power to charge the iPod touch battery, and it's slower than molasses for syncing on a subzero morning.

Don't use another USB device in a chain and don't use a USB 2.0 hub to connect your iPod touch unless the hub is a *powered* hub — a hub with a separate power source, in other words. Note that a USB keyboard typically acts like a USB 1.1 hub, but it's not powered, so it can't provide power to the iPod touch.

After adding power, your iPod touch comes alive and displays the image of the USB cable and the iTunes icon. This is a simple message telling you to connect the iPod touch to iTunes on your computer.

iTunes is the software that manages your library of content and apps on your computer, and enables you to sync apps, content, and personal information with your iPod touch, as well as update the iPod touch software and restore it to original factory settings if you need to.

Macs already have iTunes, and setting up iTunes on a Windows PC is a quick and easy process. The most up-to-date version of iTunes as of this writing is version 8.2. However, software updates occur very rapidly. If you really want the latest version, go directly to the Apple Web site (www.apple.com/itunes) to get it. You can download iTunes for free.

For details on how to install iTunes, see the instructions on Apple's Web site or see my other book, *iPod & iTunes For Dummies*.

Be aware that, for your new iPod touch and iTunes to play nice with each other, you first have to get iTunes to recognize your new device; they have to be introduced, in other words. You do that by using the Register and Set Up screen, as spelled out in the following steps:

1. **With iTunes open, connect your iPod touch to the computer with a USB cable.**

   iTunes recognizes the iPod touch and opens the Register and Set Up screen to get you started.

   If the iPod touch isn't recognized in a few minutes, make sure it's charged. A lightning bolt battery icon appears when it's asleep and connected to power — if you don't see this icon, iPod touch isn't charging properly, and you may need to try a different cable or try a different USB 2.0 connection. (For more battery details, see the section "Facing Charges of Battery" in this chapter.) If the iPod touch is charged and still not recognized, try putting it to sleep and waking it again (see the preceding section). If that doesn't make your iPod touch recognizable by iTunes, try resetting your iPod touch as described in Chapter 14. If all else fails, try restarting your computer, and if that doesn't help, try re-installing iTunes. Finally, contact Apple Support to return your iPod touch for repair (www.apple.com/support).

2. **Click Continue (or click Register Later to skip the registration process).**

   iTunes displays the License Agreement. You can scroll down to read it if you want. You must choose to accept the agreement, or the installer goes no further. (If you click to Register Later, you get to skip a few screens in the set-up process, but you don't get to skip the license agreement.)

   I don't recommend skipping the registration screens unless you intend to register the device later; registration helps you get better service from Apple in case you need it.

3. **Click the option to accept the terms at the end of the License Agreement and then click Continue.**

   After clicking Continue, iTunes lets you register your iPod touch with Apple online so you can take advantage of Apple support. You see a screen for entering your Apple ID; a membership ID for the MobileMe (formerly .Mac) service is also valid.

4. **Select the option (Use My Apple ID to Register My iPod or I Do Not Have an Apple ID) that applies to you and fill in the info beneath that option.**

   How you handle this step depends on how you purchased your iPod touch. Here's the scoop:

- If you purchased your iPod touch directly from Apple and you have an Apple Store or MobileMe ID, select the Use My Apple ID to Register My iPod option and enter the ID and password to swiftly move through the registration process. Apple automatically recognizes your purchase so that you don't need to enter the serial number.

- If you bought your iPod touch elsewhere or you don't have an Apple ID or MobileMe ID, select the I Do Not Have an Apple ID option. If needed, select your country from the pop-up menu below that. When you click Continue, iTunes displays a screen for entering your iPod touch serial number and your personal information. Fields marked with an asterisk (*) are required, such as your name and e-mail address.

Got a magnifying glass? You can find the iPod touch serial number on the back of the device or on the side of its packaging.

5. **Click Continue to advance through each screen in the registration process and click Submit at the end to submit your information.**

   After clicking Submit, iTunes displays a screen that lets you enter a name for your iPod touch, as shown in Figure 1-4.

Figure 1-4: Name your iPod touch and automatically synchronize content in one step.

If you've synchronized an iPod touch or iPhone previously on the same computer, iTunes displays an extra screen that lets you either restore settings from a previously backed-up iPod or iPhone, or you can set this iPod touch up as a new one. Choose which option you prefer and then click Continue.

6. **Give your iPod touch a name, set the automatic options, and then click Done (on a Mac) or Finish (on Windows).**

   It's nice to give your iPod touch a name to give it more of a personality. And when it comes to setting automatic options (refer to Figure 1-4), here's the deal:

   - *Automatically Sync Songs and Videos:* If you want to copy your entire iTunes music and video library onto your iPod touch, leave the Automatically Sync Songs and Videos option selected. If you want to control which portion of your library is copied to the iPod touch, deselect this option and turn to Chapter 5 for synchronization details.

   - *Automatically Add Photos:* Select this option to copy all the photos in your Pictures folder or photo library to your iPod touch. (See Chapter 9 for information about synchronizing photo libraries.) Leave it deselected if you want to transfer photos later.

   - *Automatically Sync Applications:* Select this option to copy all iPod touch apps in your iTunes library to your iPod touch.

Don't want to add songs or videos now? If you deselect the option to automatically synchronize (refer to Figure 1-4), you can still add songs and videos later, along with podcasts and audio books — either manually or automatically, as I describe in Chapter 5.

After finishing setup, your iPod touch name appears in the iTunes Source pane (the left column) under the Devices heading (refer to Figure 1-6). Click this name to display information about your iPod touch in the main part of the iTunes window. The information you see also includes a message to update your iPod touch if Apple has an update for it. If you see this message, click the Update button to update your iPod touch. If you have an earlier model iPod touch, you can download the iPhone Software update (sold seperately) to bring it up to date. See Chapter 14 for details.

If you chose the option to automatically synchronize your songs and videos, your iPod touch quickly fills up with music and videos from your iTunes library.

You can leave your iPod touch connected to the computer, using the computer as a source of power — the iPod touch appears in iTunes whenever you start iTunes.

To disconnect it from iTunes and your computer, click the eject button next to the iPod touch name (refer to Figure 1-4) in the Source pane. (The eject button shows a triangle with a line beneath it.)

After ejecting the iPod touch, wait for its display to show the Home screen or the slider to unlock it (or for it to go to sleep, which it should do in a few minutes). You can then disconnect the iPod touch from the computer. Don't ever disconnect an iPod touch before ejecting it because such bad behavior might cause it to freeze up and require a reset. (If that happens, see Chapter 14 for instructions.)

Facing Charges of Battery

You can take a six-hour flight from New York City to California and listen to your iPod touch the entire time — and with some models, listen all the way back on the return flight — without recharging. The iPod touch uses a built-in, rechargeable lithium-ion (Li-Ion) battery that offers 36 hours of music playing time or 6 hours of video, browsing the Internet, or displaying photo slideshows with music.

Recharging your battery

The iPod touch battery recharges automatically when you connect it to a power source. For example, it starts charging immediately when you insert it into a dock that's connected to a power source (or to a computer with a powered USB connection). It takes only four hours to recharge the battery fully.

Need power when you're on the run? Look for a power outlet in the airport terminal or hotel lobby and plug in your iPod touch with your AC power adapter — the battery fast-charges to 80 percent capacity in two hours. After that, the battery receives a trickle charge for the next two hours until it's fully charged.

Don't fry your iPod touch with some generic power adapter. Use *only* the power adapter from Apple or a certified iPod adapter, such as the power accessories from Belkin, Griffin, Monster, XtremeMac, and other vendors.

When you awaken an iPod touch that's plugged into power, you see a large battery icon indicating how much juice you have. When you charge the battery, the large battery icon includes a lightning bolt.

You can also use your iPod touch while the battery is charging, or you can disconnect it and use it before the battery is fully charged. The small battery icon in the top-right corner of the iPod touch display indicates how much power is left. It's completely filled in when the battery is fully charged, and it slowly empties out into just an outline as the battery is used up. A lightning bolt appears inside it when recharging, and a plug appears inside when the iPod touch is connected to power.

The iPod touch built-in, rechargeable battery is, essentially, a life-or-death proposition. After it's dead, it can be replaced, but Apple charges a replacement fee plus shipping. If your warranty is still active, you should have Apple replace it under the warranty program (which may cost nothing except perhaps shipping). Don't try to replace it yourself because opening your iPod touch invalidates the warranty.

Keeping an iPod touch in a snug carrying case when charging is tempting but also potentially disastrous. You could damage the unit by overheating it and frying its circuits, rendering it as useful as a paperweight. To get around this problem, you can purchase one of the heat-dissipating carrying cases available in the Apple Store.

If you don't use your iPod touch for a month, even while it's connected to power and retaining a charge, it can become catatonic. Perhaps it gets depressed from being left alone too long. At that point it may not start — you have to completely drain and recharge the battery. To drain the battery, leave your iPod touch unconnected to power for 24 hours. Then, to fully recharge the battery, connect it to power for at least 4 hours without using it (or longer if you are using it).

Saving power

The iPod touch uses power accessing the Internet, using Bluetooth devices, and running apps. Keeping these activities to a minimum can help you save power.

The following are tips on saving power while using your iPod touch:

- ✔ **Pause.** Pause playback when you're not listening. Pausing (stopping) playback is the easiest way to conserve power.

- ✔ **Lock it.** Press the Sleep/Wake button on top of the iPod touch to immediately put it to sleep and lock its controls to save battery power. You can set your iPod touch to automatically go to sleep by choosing Settings⇨General⇨Auto-Lock from the Home screen, and choosing 1 Minute, 2 Minutes, 3 Minutes, 4 Minutes, or 5 Minutes (or Never, to prevent automatic sleep).

- ✔ **Back away from the light.** Turn down the brightness on an iPod touch by choosing Settings⇨Brightness and dragging the brightness slider to the left.

✔ **Forget where you are.** Turn off Location Services if you aren't using apps that need it. Choose Settings⇨General from the Home screen, and touch On for the Location Services option to turn it off. See Chapter 3 for details.

✔ **Let the postman ring twice.** Check e-mail less frequently. You may want to change Push and Fetch settings to be less frequent. See Chapter 11 for details.

✔ **Put a cap on Bluetooth.** Turn off Bluetooth (choose Settings⇨General⇨Bluetooth and touch the On button to turn it off) if you're not using a Bluetooth device. (Bluetooth is available only with the iPhone 3 Software Update.)

✔ **Stop communicating altogether.** Turn off Wi-Fi when not browsing the Internet: Choose Settings⇨Wi-Fi and touch the On button to turn it off.

✔ **Turn it off completely.** You can turn the iPod touch completely off by holding down the Sleep/Wake (On/Off) button for about two seconds, until you see the Slide to Power Off slider; then slide your finger across the slider to turn it off. You can then turn it back on by pressing and holding the Sleep/Wake (On/Off) button.

Keep in mind that starting up an iPod touch that was completely turned off takes quite a bit of power — more than if it woke from sleep. If you do turn it off, plug it into AC power or your computer before turning it back on.

✔ **You may continue.** Play songs continuously without using the iPod touch controls. Selecting songs and using Previous/Rewind and Next/Fast-Forward require more energy. Also, turn off your iPod touch equalizer (EQ) if you turned it on (see Chapter 7).

Always use the latest iPod touch software and update your software when updates come out. Apple constantly tries to improve how your iPod touch works, and many of these advancements relate to power usage.

Putting Your Finger On It

*W*ith an iPod touch, your fingers do the walking. The multi-touch glass screen lets you make gestures to do things, such as flicking a finger to scroll a list quickly, sliding your finger to scroll slowly or to drag a slider (such as the volume slider), pinching with two fingers to zoom out of a Web page in Safari, or pulling apart with two fingers (also known as *unpinching*) to zoom in to the page to see it more clearly.

This chapter gives you a quick tour of the iPod touch Home screen and icons, and it describes all the touch-and-gesture tricks to make your iPod touch dance and sing. I also give you a complete tour of the most unique feature of the iPod touch: the onscreen keyboard.

Going on a Quick Tour of the iPod touch

The iPod touch responds to tapping, flicking, and sliding your finger, among other gestures (such as shaking, tilting, two-finger tapping, and so on). One tap is all you need to run an app or select something, but sometimes you have to slide your finger to scroll the display and see more selections.

Sticky fingers are not recommended. To clean your iPod touch, make sure to unplug all cables and turn it off. (See Chapter 1.) Use a soft, slightly damp, lint-free cloth to wipe your iPod touch clean — see Chapter 15 for cleaning tips.

Sliding to the Home screen

The first message you see on an iPod touch display (besides the time of day and the date) is `Slide to unlock` — to get started, you have to unlock the iPod touch by sliding your finger across the message. Once unlocked, your Home screen appears in all its glory. (See Figure 2-1.)

There's no place like Home — it's the screen where you start. Everything is available from the Home screen at the touch of a finger (see Figure 2-1). For example:

- Tap the Music icon to access your music.
- Tap the Videos icon to access your videos.
- Tap the Photos icon to access your photos.
- Tap the iTunes icon to access the iTunes Store.
- Tap the App Store icon to access the App Store.

Figure 2-1: The iPod touch Home screen.

After tapping an icon on the iPod touch screen, a new screen appears with selections and icons. (Touching Music, for example, brings up Artists, Songs, Albums, and so on.) The multi-touch interface changes for each app. Press the physical Home button below the screen at any time to go to back to the Home screen.

Apps you download from the App Store (as I describe in Chapter 4) show up as icons on your Home screen. You can also save Web Clips to your Home screen as icons that take you directly to those Web pages (as I describe in Chapter 10). When you add enough apps and Web Clips so that they no longer all fit on the first page of the Home screen, the iPod touch automatically creates more Home screen pages to accommodate them.

The bottom row of the Home screen (the one holding the Safari, Music, Videos, and App Store icons, as shown in Figure 2-1) is called the *dock.* The number of dots above the dock shows the number of Home screen pages you have, and it indicates which page you're viewing. To switch to another Home screen page, flick with your finger left or right, or tap to the left or right of the row of dots.

You can also create additional Home screens yourself. Touch and hold any icon until all the icons begin to wiggle. (That's right, it looks like they're doing the Wa-Wa-Watusi.) Then drag a wiggling icon to the right edge of the screen until a new page appears. You can flick to return to the original Home screen page and drag more wiggling icons to the new page. You can create up to nine Home screen pages.

Press the Home button under the screen to go to back to the first Home screen.

While the wiggling icons are doing their show, you can also rearrange them. Drag the wiggling icons into new positions, and the other icons move to accommodate, creating a new arrangement.

You can also delete apps you downloaded from the App Store by tapping the circled X that appears inside the icon as it wiggles.

To stop all that wiggling, press the Home button, which saves your new arrangement and pages.

To reset your Home screen to the default arrangement, thereby cleaning up any mess you may have made on your Home screens, tap Settings⇨General⇨Reset⇨Reset Home Screen Layout.

Status bar

The iPod touch shows its current state in the status bar at the top of the screen (refer to Figure 2-1). The icons mean the following:

- **iPod:** Just in case you forgot you had an iPod in your hands (very existential).

- **Wi-Fi:** This icon says the iPod touch is connected to a Wi-Fi network. If the network offers Internet access (all commercial ones do), you're on the Internet. The more bars you see in the icon, the stronger the connection to the network. To find out more about setting up Wi-Fi with Internet in your home, see Chapter 4.

- **Network activity:** This icon twirls to show that data is traveling from the network to your iPod touch (or vice versa). (Not visible in Figure 2-1.)

- **VPN:** If you have special network settings that access a virtual private network (VPN), this icon shows up to tell you that you are connected to it. See Chapter 4 for details. (Not visible in Figure 2-1.)

- **Lock:** You see this icon whenever the iPod touch is locked. (The Slide to unlock message also appears on the screen.) (Not visible in Figure 2-1.)

✔ **Play:** This icon tells you that a song, audio book, or podcast is playing (in case you didn't know — maybe you took your headphones off). (Not visible in Figure 2-1.)

✔ **Alarm:** This icon appears if you set an alarm. See Chapter 3 for details. (Not visible in Figure 2-1.)

✔ **Battery:** The Battery icon shows the battery level or charging status. It's completely filled in when the battery is fully charged, and it slowly empties out into just an outline as the battery is used up. A lightning bolt appears inside the icon when the device is recharging, and a plug appears inside it when the iPod touch is connected to power.

Searching for anything

The leftmost dot above the dock (refer to Figure 2-1) is a search icon. Tap the search icon (or flick the Home screen with your finger to the right) to show the Spotlight Search screen (Figure 2-2). Spotlight Search works just like the Spotlight universal search in Mac OS X. You can type a search term and immediately see suggestions.

Search looks through contacts, calendars, e-mail (the To:, From:, and Subject: fields, but not the message content), the content (songs, videos, podcasts, and audio books), and even the text in the Notes app. Tap a contact, calendar entry, e-mail, or note suggestion to open it, or tap the song, video, podcast, or audio book suggestion to play it.

Figure 2-2: The iPod touch Search screen.

Tons of icons and what do you get?

You get flexible apps and a key to the net! The iPod touch Home screen (refer to Figure 2-1) offers the following icons:

✔ **Safari:** Use the Safari Web browser.

✔ **Calendar:** View your calendar.

✔ **Mail:** Check and send e-mail.

- **Contacts:** View your contacts.

- **YouTube:** List and select videos from YouTube.

- **Stocks:** Check the prices for financial stocks, bonds, and funds.

- **Maps:** View maps and get driving directions.

- **Weather:** View the weather in multiple cities.

- **Clock:** View multiple clocks and use the alarm clock, timer, and stopwatch.

- **Calculator:** You can use your iPod touch as a regular calculator for adding, subtracting, multiplying, dividing, and so on. Also, if you hold the iPod touch horizontally, it becomes a scientific calculator.

- **Notes:** Add text notes.

- **Voice Memos:** Add voice recordings (using an external mic).

- **Settings:** Adjust settings for Wi-Fi, sounds, brightness, Safari, and other apps, as well as other settings for the iPod touch itself.

- **App Store:** Go to Apple's online App Store to download other Apple and third-party apps.

- **Music:** Select music playlists, artists, songs, albums, and more (including podcasts, genres, composers, audio books, and compilations). The Music icon also offers Cover Flow browsing, as I describe in Chapter 7.

- **Videos:** Select videos by type (movies, music videos, TV shows, or video podcasts).

- **Photos:** Select photos by photo album or select individual photos in the Photo Library.

- **iTunes:** Go to the iTunes online store to purchase content.

There's one more icon for an app that you can activate in Settings, if you have the appropriate Nike shoes and the Nike+ iPod Sport Kit, sold separately. See Chapter 15 for details.

Touching and Gesturing

With the iPod touch, it's touch and go. The iPod touch responds to the following gestures you make with your fingers:

- **Drag with your finger:** Scroll up or down lists slowly.

- **Flick up or down:** Swipe your finger quickly across the surface to scroll up or down lists rapidly.

- **Touch and hold:** While scrolling, touch and hold to stop the moving list.

- **Flick from left to right or right to left:** Quickly swipe your finger across the screen to change screens or application panes (Home screens, Cover Flow view in Music, Weather, and other apps).
- **Single tap:** Select an item.
- **Double tap:** Zoom in or out with Safari, Maps, and other applications.
- **Two-finger single tap:** Zoom out in Maps.
- **Pinch:** Zoom out.
- **Unpinch:** Zoom in.

Need to practice your tapping? Try Tap Tap Revenge, a rhythm game that plays music while requiring you to tap each of the colored balls when they reach the line at the bottom of the screen. If you tap the ball on the beat, you gain points; if not, it counts as a miss. You can also activate a revenge mode to score more points by shaking the iPod touch after setting a winning streak of 50 beats.

Shake, rattle, and roll

Your iPod touch can sense motion using a built-in accelerometer. When you rotate it from a vertical view (portrait) to a horizontal view (landscape), the accelerometer detects the movement and changes the display accordingly. This happens so quickly that you can control a game with these movements.

For example, Pass the Pigs is a dice game in which you shake three times to roll your pigs to gain points. In the Labyrinth game, you tilt your iPod touch to roll a ball through a wooden maze without falling through the holes. And you can shake, rattle, and roll your way around the world in Yahtzee Adventures as you rack up high scores.

And if that's too tame for you, try Chopper, a helicopter game in which you need to complete your mission and return to base while avoiding enemy fire from tanks and bazooka-wielding madmen. You tilt the iPod touch to fly, and you touch the screen to drop bombs or fire the machine gun.

Xhake Shake lets you shake, flip, rub, and tap your iPod touch to challenge your hand-eye responses. And for scrolling practice, try Light Bike (loosely based on the Disney movie *Tron*) in which you scroll to maneuver a light bike from a third-person perspective against three computer-controlled light bikes. And infants can join the fun: Silver Rattle shows a screen that changes color and rattles with every shake. Big Joe Turner would be proud.

Tickling the Keyboard

One trick that's sure to amaze your friends is the ability to whip out your iPod touch and type notes, contact information, calendar entries, map locations, stock symbols, and even the addresses for Web sites. You can also make selections for pop-up menus. You can do all this with the onscreen keyboard.

You may want to start practicing on the keyboard with just one finger, and as you get used to it, try also using your thumb. Tap a text entry field, such as the URL field for a Web page in Safari (as I describe in Chapter 10) or the text of an e-mail message (as I describe in Chapter 11), and the onscreen keyboard appears.

Typing text, numbers, and symbols (using Notes)

You can practice your technique using the Notes app. Tap Notes on the Home screen, and the onscreen keyboard appears with letters of the alphabet, as shown in Figure 2-3 on the left. (If you've already saved notes, a list of notes appears — tap the + button in the upper-right corner to type a new note.)

Tap the keys, and as you type, each letter appears above your thumb or finger. If you tap the wrong key, slide your finger to the correct key. The letter isn't entered until you lift your finger from the key.

Figure 2-3: Type characters (left) and numbers (right).

To enter numbers, symbols, or punctuation, tap the .?123 key at the bottom-left corner of the keyboard (refer to Figure 2-3, left side), which changes the keyboard layout to numbers (refer to Figure 2-3, right side). After tapping the .?123 key, you can then tap the #+= key to change the keyboard layout to symbols. To return to the alphabetical keys, tap the ABC key.

You can start a new sentence quickly by double-tapping the spacebar to insert a period followed by a space. The keyboard automatically capitalizes the next word after you type a period, a question mark, or an exclamation point.

To enable caps lock (locking the keyboard to uppercase letters), choose Settings⇨General⇨Keyboard and then tap the Off button next to Enable Caps Lock to turn it on. (Tap it again to turn it off.) You can then double-tap the Shift key to turn on lock caps (uppercase letters). The Shift key turns blue, and all letters you type are uppercase. Tap the Shift key again to turn caps lock off.

To save your note, tap Done in the upper-right corner. A list of Notes appears with a date attached to each note. You can also delete a note by choosing the note and tapping the trash icon at the bottom of the note.

You can transfer notes you type in Notes to your computer by e-mailing them to yourself. Choose the note from the Notes screen and tap the envelope icon at the bottom of the note to display a ready-made e-mail message containing the text of your note — all you need to do is enter the e-mail address. See Chapter 11 for details on sending the message.

Here's a trick you can use to switch to the numeric keyboard layout and back to alphabetical layout automatically, in order to type a number and continue typing letters: Touch and hold down the .?123 key and then slide your finger over the keyboard to the number you want. Release your finger to select the number. The onscreen keyboard reverts back immediately to alphabetical keys so that you can continue typing letters.

Need to use an accent mark? For instance, the word *café* should really have an accent mark over the *e,* and there may even come a day when you need to include a foreign word or two in a note — lycée or Autowäsche or también, for example. Although you can switch the language for the keyboard (as I describe in Chapter 15), you can also include an accent mark over a vowel by using the English keyboard. Hold your finger on a vowel (such as *e*) to show a row of keys that offer variations on the letter. Slide your finger over the row to highlight the variation you want and then release your finger to select it.

Editing text and handling word suggestions

Yes, you can edit your mistakes. To edit text in an entry field, touch and hold to see the magnifier, which magnifies portions of the text view as shown in Figure 2-4 (left side).

Figure 2-4: Touch and hold for the magnifier (left) and release when positioned correctly (right).

Before releasing your finger, slide the magnifier to the position for inserting text. After releasing, the Select/Select All/Paste bubble appears above the insertion point, as shown in Figure 2-4 (right side), which is useful for selecting, copying, and pasting text (as I describe in the next section). You can then tap keys to insert text, or you can use the backspace key — the key sporting the X — to remove text.

The intelligent keyboard automatically suggests corrections as you type, as shown in Figure 2-5 (some languages only). You don't need to accept the suggested word — just continue typing. If you do want to accept it, tap the spacebar, a punctuation mark, or the Return key. iPod touch fills in the rest of the word.

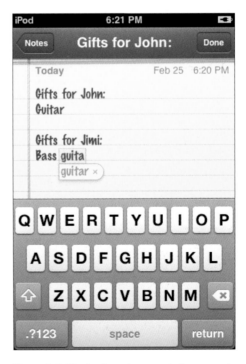

Figure 2-5: The keyboard suggests the correct word for a typo.

To reject the suggested word, finish typing the word or tap the *x* next to the suggestion to dismiss it. Each time you reject a suggestion for the same word, your iPod touch keeps track and eventually adds the word you've been using all along to its dictionary. The iPod touch includes dictionaries for English, English (UK), French, French (Canada), German, Japanese, Spanish, Italian, Dutch, and other languages. The appropriate dictionary is activated automatically when you select an international keyboard. (See Chapter 15 for details about international keyboards.)

You can turn off suggestions by choosing Settings➪General➪Keyboard from the Home screen and tapping On for Auto-Correction. (On changes to Off when you tap it.)

Copying (or cutting) and pasting

You can copy or cut a chunk of text and paste it into another app — for example, you can copy a paragraph from a note in Notes and paste it into an e-mail message in Mail, or vice-versa. You can even copy paragraphs from a Web page and paste them in Notes or an e-mail message, as I show in Chapter 10.

To select the nearest word (or even the entire text) for copying or cutting, touch an insertion point to bring up the magnifier, then release to show the Select/Select All/Paste bubble. (Refer to Figure 2-4, right side.) You can then tap Select to select the nearest word or tap Select All to select all of the text. The Cut/Copy/Paste bubble appears above the text, which is selected with handles on either end, as shown in Figure 2-6 (left side). Tap Cut to cut the selection, or Copy to copy it.

To paste the cut or copied text somewhere new, open a note (or create a new note) in Notes, or start a new e-mail message, or open any app that lets you enter text. Touch and hold to magnify the text view so that you can mark an insertion point precisely. After you remove your finger, the Cut/Copy/Paste bubble appears, or if the message or note already contains text, the Select/Select All/Paste bubble appears, as shown in Figure 2-6 (right side). Either way, you can then tap Paste to paste the text at the insertion point.

You can also double-tap a word to select it for copying (or cutting) and pasting. You can also make a more precise selection by dragging one of the handles. A rectangular magnifier appears for dragging the handle precisely. After you remove your finger to stop dragging, the Cut/Copy/Paste bubble appears for copying (or cutting) the selection.

Setting keyboard options

To set keyboard options, choose Settings➪General➪Keyboard from the Home screen. The Keyboard settings screen appears, with options for Auto-Correction, Auto-Capitalization, Enable Caps Lock, and the Shortcut for inserting a period.

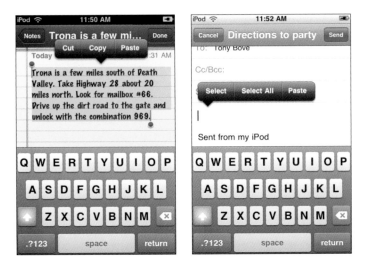

Figure 2-6: Copy or cut the selected text (left), and paste into a message (right).

Tap On to turn off Auto-Correction if you don't want the keyboard to suggest typing corrections.

Auto-Capitalization automatically capitalizes the next word after you type a period, question mark, or exclamation point (punctuation that ends a sentence). It also automatically capitalizes after you tap the Return key. The assumption is that you're starting a new sentence or new line of text that should begin with a capital letter. Tap On to turn this feature off if you want; tap Off to turn it back on.

To turn on caps lock (locking the keyboard to upper case letters), tap the Off button next to Enable Caps Lock. (Tap it again to turn it off.) You can then double-tap the Shift key to turn on caps lock (uppercase letters). The Shift key turns blue, and all letters you type are uppercase. Tap the Shift key again to turn caps lock off.

The Shortcut for inserting a period is to double-tap the spacebar, which inserts a period followed by a space. The assumption is that you want to finish a sentence and start the next one. Tap On to turn this feature off if you want; tap Off to turn it back on.

3

Clocking, Locking, and Personalizing

*Y*ou may think Apple designed the iPod touch just for listening to music or watching videos, but those thoughtful engineers crammed a lot more features into their invention. You can use your iPod touch as a time-keeper to help you keep track of your personal life — setting alarms, using the stopwatch, and displaying clocks of different time zones for traveling. And if you worry that your iPod touch might fall into the wrong hands, consider setting a combination lock. This chapter shows you how to do all this and more with your iPod touch: Find out how to set the brightness of the display, set the *wallpaper* (a stylin' background when it's locked), turn on its capability to know your location, and set restrictions on downloading and playing content.

There's No Time Like the Right Time

Your iPod touch may already be set to the correct time, date, and time zone, but if not, you can set it yourself and even set how the time appears in the status bar at the top of the screen. To set the date and time, follow these steps:

1. **Choose Settings⇨General⇨Date & Time from the Home screen.**

   The Date & Time screen appears with the 24-Hour Time, Time Zone, Set Date & Time options, and time zone support for your calendar.

2. **(Optional) Tap the Off button for the 24-Hour Time option to turn it on and show military time.**

   With 24-hour display, 11 p.m. is displayed as 23:00:00 and not 11:00:00. To turn off the 24-Hour Time option, tap the On button.

3. **Tap the Time Zone option to set the time zone.**

   The onscreen keyboard appears; see Chapter 2 for instructions on how to use it. Type the name of the city you're in (or, if you're in the middle of nowhere, the nearest big city) and tap the Return button on the keyboard, and your iPod touch looks up the time zone for you.

4. **Tap the Date & Time button in the upper-left corner of the display to finish and return to the Date & Time menu.**

5. **Tap the Set Date & Time option.**

   Tapping the Date field brings up a slot-machine-style Date wheel, as shown in Figure 3-1.

6. **Slide your finger over the wheel to select the month, day, and year.**

   Slide until the selection you want appears in the gray window on the slot-machine wheel.

7. **Tap the Time field to bring up a Time wheel. Slide your finger over the wheel to set the hour, minutes, and AM or PM.**

Figure 3-1: Slide the wheel of fortune to set the month, day, year (left) and time (right).

8. **Tap the Date & Time button in the upper-left corner of the display (refer to Figure 3-1) to finish and return to the Date & Time menu.**

9. **Tap the General button in the upper-left corner to return to the General screen.**

Rock Around the Clocks

You can always know what time it is with your iPod touch — just look at the time on the Home screen. But you can also know what time it is in other time zones by displaying multiple clocks. Your iPod touch even lets you set alarms and run a stopwatch.

Checking the time in Paris and Bangkok

You can display clocks with different time zones, which is useful for traveling halfway around the world (or calling someone who lives halfway around the world).

To create clocks, tap the Clock icon on the Home screen and tap the World Clock icon along the bottom of the display. It takes only two steps to add a clock:

1. **Touch the plus (+) button in the upper-right corner of the display.**

   The onscreen keyboard appears with a text entry field.

2. **Type a city name on the keyboard and tap Return (or tap Cancel next to the text entry field to cancel).**

   The iPod touch looks up the city's time zone to display the clock. (For details on how to use the onscreen keyboard, see Chapter 2.)

The initial clock and any clocks you add sport a daytime face (white background and black hands) from 6 a.m. to 5:59 p.m., as shown in Figure 3-2, and a nighttime face (black background with white hands) from 6 p.m. to 5:59 a.m.

Figure 3-2: Add a clock for any time zone.

To remove a clock, tap the Edit button in the upper-left corner of the display (refer to Figure 3-2) and then tap the circled minus (–) button next to the clock to delete.

Getting alarmed

Time is on your side with your iPod touch. You can set *multiple* alarms to go off on different days and set a variety of tones and sounds for your alarms that play through its speaker. Follow these steps:

1. **Tap the Clock icon on the Home screen and tap the Alarm icon along the bottom of the display.**

2. **To add an alarm, tap the plus (+) button in the upper-right corner of the display.**

   The Add Alarm screen appears, as shown in Figure 3-3, with options and a slot-machine-style wheel for setting the alarm time.

3. **Slide your finger over the wheel to set the hour and minute, and AM or PM.**

   Slide until the selection you want appears in the gray window on the slot-machine wheel.

   Now you can set some optional features, or you can skip to Step 8 and be done with it.

4. **(Optional) Tap the Repeat option to set the alarm to repeat on other days.**

   You can set it to repeat every Monday, Tuesday, Wednesday, Thursday, Friday, Saturday, or Sunday.

5. **(Optional) Tap the Sound option to select a sound for the alarm.**

   A list of sounds appears; touch a sound to set it for the alarm.

Figure 3-3: Add an alarm.

6. **(Optional) Tap the On button to turn off the Snooze option, or tap it again to turn it back on.**

   With the Snooze option, the iPod touch displays a Snooze button when the alarm goes off, and you tap Snooze to stop the alarm and have it repeat in 10 minutes (so that you can snooze for 10 minutes).

7. **(Optional) Tap the Label option to enter a text label for the alarm.**

   The label helps you identify the alarm in the Alarm list.

8. **Tap the Save button in the upper-right corner to save the alarm.**

When the alarm goes off, your iPod touch displays the message `You have an alarm` (and the date and time), along with the Snooze button if the Snooze option is turned on (refer to Step 6). Slide your finger to unlock the iPod touch to stop the alarm's sound, or tap the Snooze button to stop the alarm temporarily and let it repeat 10 minutes later. (When it goes off again, slide the unlock slider to turn it off — don't tap the Snooze button again, you're late for work!)

To delete an alarm, tap the Clock icon on the Home screen and tap the Alarm icon along the bottom of the display. In the Alarm list, tap the alarm you want to trash and then tap the Edit button in the upper-left corner of the display. The alarm appears with a circled minus (–) button next to it; tap this button and then tap the red Delete button that appears to delete the alarm.

Timing your steps

You can set an hour-and-minute timer for anything — baking cookies, baking CDs, or baking in the sun on the beach. The timer built into the Clock app will continue running even when playing music or videos or running other iPod touch apps. You might want to use a timer to see whether a set of activities — playing songs, playing videos, selecting from menus, and running apps — occurs within a specific time. (If you need to use seconds as well as minutes and hours, try the stopwatch, which I describe later in this section.)

To use the timer, follow these steps:

1. **Tap the Clock icon on the Home screen.**

   The Clock display appears.

2. **Tap the Timer icon along the bottom of the Clock display.**

   The Timer wheel for minutes and hours appears, along with the Start button.

3. **Flick the timer wheel to set the timer in hours and minutes.**

4. **Tap the When Timer Ends button and tap a sound to use when the timer is up.**

5. **Tap Set in the upper-right corner of the display to set the sound (or Cancel in the upper-left corner to cancel the sound).**

6. **Tap Start to start the timer.**

The timer runs backward. You can touch Cancel to cancel the timer or wait until it runs out. When it runs out, the iPod touch plays the sound (if a sound is set) and presents an OK button. Tap OK to stop the sound.

Let the good times roll

Lots of games use the iPod touch clock to measure time. Some use it against you: Super Horsey (see the vertical figure with the chess piece) is a very challenging game that puts you in the role of the traditional chess knight who must complete the labyrinth before the time elapses.

If speed is the issue, SlotZ Racer lets up to four people race slot cars on a single iPod touch. You can compete for laps or against the clock in Time Trials and drive an endurance race (with simulated days and nights). SlotZ Track Editor lets you create the slot-car track of your dreams, with huge and detailed tracks that you can trick out with jumps, bridges, and scenery.

If you enjoy role-playing games that take you on a journey with humor and storytelling (like Zelda, Pokemon, Dragon Quest, or Final Fantasy), try Arvale: Journey of Illusion, which offers over 20 hours of game-play, six immense continents, 280 maps (see the horizontal figure with a map), 200 monsters, hundreds of items (including wheelbarrows), and thousands of laughs. And in Rock'n'Roll, you've messed up your enemy's music game, and all the notes have scattered over an island — it's up to you to roll through each level to collect these notes. Once all the notes are collected, you move on to the next level. But in Rock the Clock mode, there are another 15 levels that must be beaten in the time provided. Good luck with that!

Using the stopwatch

You can use a stopwatch with a lap timer for timing exercises, jogging, race laps, how long it takes the bus to travel across town, or how long your friend takes to recognize the song you're playing. Whatever you want to measure with accurate time to the tenth of a second, the stopwatch is ready for you.

Even while you're running the stopwatch, you can still use the iPod touch to play music, videos, audio books, and podcasts. When you play a video, the stopwatch continues to count as usual; when you switch back to the stopwatch display, the video automatically pauses.

To use the stopwatch, follow these steps:

1. **Tap the Clock icon on the Home screen and tap the Stopwatch icon along the bottom of the display.**

   A stopwatch appears with Start and Reset buttons and 00:00.00 (minutes, seconds, and fractions of seconds) as the stopwatch counter.

2. **Tap the Start button to start counting.**

   The stopwatch starts counting immediately, while the left button changes to Stop, and the right button changes to Lap, as shown in Figure 3-4.

3. **(Optional) Tap the Lap button to mark each lap.**

   Tap the Lap button to record each lap. Repeat this step for each lap.

Figure 3-4: After tapping Start (left) and after tapping Lap (right).

4. **Tap the Stop button to stop counting.**

   The counter stops counting. The left button changes to Start, and the right button changes to Reset. You can resume the count from where you left off by tapping Start, or you can start the count again from zero by tapping Reset.

Setting the Passcode for Your Lock

Your iPod touch locks itself when it goes to sleep, and, as you already know, you have to slide your finger over the unlock message to wake it up. But you can also set a four-digit combination passcode that keeps the iPod touch from waking up unless you supply the passcode. *Note:* The lock-up works only when your iPod touch is not attached to a computer.

If you're playing music when you lock your iPod touch, the music continues playing — and you can even use the Play/Pause button to pause and resume playback — but if you set a passcode, no one can navigate the iPod touch or even change the volume without providing the combination.

To conserve power, you can force your iPod touch to go to sleep by pressing the Sleep/Wake (On/Off) button, but it won't unlock. When it awakes, it remembers everything — including the passcode you need to provide.

Don't bother to call Apple to see whether the company can unlock your iPod touch for you. If you can't attach it to the proper computer or enter the correct passcode combination, your only recourse is to restore the iPod touch to its factory conditions — see Chapter 14.

To set a combination passcode, follow these steps:

1. **Choose Settings⇨General⇨Passcode Lock from the Home screen.**

   The Set Passcode display appears.

2. **Enter a four-number passcode by tapping numbers on the calculator-style keypad.**

   If you change your mind, tap the Cancel button to cancel the operation.

3. **Enter the same passcode number again to confirm the passcode.**

   After entering the passcode again, the Passcode Lock menu appears with the Turn Passcode Off, Change Passcode, and Require Passcode options.

4. **Select the Passcode option you want to use.**

   You can turn off the passcode, change it, or set the Require Passcode option to Immediately, After 1 Minute, After 5 Minutes, After 15 Minutes, After 1 Hour, or After 4 Hours.

5. **When you're done, tap General to return to the General menu.**

Don't forget this combination! Use a four-digit number that's easy to commit to memory.

To unlock a passcode-locked iPod touch, you must do one of the following:

- ✓ **Enter the same combination.** After correctly entering the combination, the iPod touch unlocks and returns to the last viewed screen.

- ✓ **Attach the iPod touch to the computer you used to synchronize it with iTunes.** When you disconnect it after synchronizing with iTunes, the iPod touch is no longer locked with a passcode.

- ✓ **Restore your iPod touch to its original factory settings.** As I describe in Chapter 14, this erases everything in the process. This is, of course, a measure of last resort.

After setting a passcode, you can set how long to wait before the passcode is required by choosing Settings⇨General⇨Passcode Lock from the Home screen and then entering your passcode. Tap Require Passcode and then select how long the iPod touch can be idle before you need to enter a passcode to unlock it.

You can also set the option to erase data after ten failed passcode attempts. Choose Settings⇨General⇨Passcode Lock from the Home screen, and then enter your passcode. Tap Erase Data to turn it on.

With the Erase Data option turned on, if anyone (including you) tries ten times to enter the passcode and fails each time, your iPod touch settings are reset to their defaults and all your information and media are removed by overwriting the data. It's as if the Mission: Impossible force had set it to self-destruct. Your iPod touch is restored to factory conditions, so you might as well go to Chapter 14 to see what that means.

Getting Personal

Your future might be so bright that you gotta wear shades, but your iPod touch display might not be bright enough. And it still needs that personal touch that only wallpaper can bring.

And of course, there are the keyboard clicks and alert sounds you can use to indicate that e-mail has arrived, that something in your calendar needs attention, and so on. Screen brightness, wallpaper, and sound effects are a lot to keep track of, but your iPod touch makes customizing each feature so doggone easy.

If you share your iPod touch with children or adults that act like children, you may want to place restrictions that prevent explicit music from the iTunes Store from being displayed in playlists, or prevent the use of apps such as YouTube, or stop any access to the iTunes Store or App Store. Your iPod touch can let you do that, too.

Brightening and wallpapering

To adjust the brightness, first tap the Settings icon on the Home screen and then tap Brightness, which is near the top of the Settings screen. The Brightness screen appears with a slider that shows the brightness setting, which ranges from low (a dim sun icon) to high (a bright sun icon). Slide the brightness slider's knob with your finger to the right to increase the brightness (toward the bright sun) and to the left to decrease the brightness (toward the dim sun). Of course, the brighter the screen, the more power it draws from the battery.

While you're at it, why not wallpaper your display? You can make your iPod touch display a stylish background when it's locked. You can also put up photos or other images from your photo library as your wallpaper.

It's not like you'll see it often — the iPod touch displays the wallpaper image only when you first press the Sleep/Wake button. After you swipe with your finger to unlock your iPod touch, the wallpaper is replaced by the Home screen or whatever app you were last running.

To set the wallpaper, choose Settings⇨General⇨Wallpaper from the Home screen. You can then choose from among stylish built-in wallpaper images by tapping the Wallpaper button.

You can also choose from the entire photo library on your iPod touch by tapping Photo Library, or you can choose saved photos by tapping Saved Photos. (For more about photos, see Chapter 9.)

Tap a thumbnail to select the image for your wallpaper or tap the Wallpaper button in the upper-left corner to return to the Wallpaper menu. After tapping an image, your iPod touch displays the Move and Scale screen, which lets you optionally pan the image by dragging your finger, and optionally zoom in or out of the image by pinching and unpinching with your fingers. Tap the Set Wallpaper button to set the image as your wallpaper or tap Cancel to cancel.

Sound effects

Don't want to hear the keyboard click as you type, or the snap noise as you swipe your finger over the "unlock" message? You can set which events can trigger sound effects as well as the volume of the sound effect.

Choose Settings⇨General⇨Sounds from the Home screen. You can then turn the alert on or off and click sounds for new mail, sent mail, calendar alerts, locking and unlocking, and using the onscreen keyboard. Tap On to turn off each option, or vice versa.

Location, location, location

Perhaps nothing is more personal than your physical location. Your iPod touch can triangulate its location with scary precision, even though it has neither a cell phone nor the location-determining technology known as GPS. (The iPod touch's cousin, the iPhone, does have both a cell phone and GPS.) The iPod touch does this by leveraging the most extensive Wi-Fi reference database in the world.

Why should you care? The Maps app can find your location on the map, which is very useful for getting directions (see Chapter 12). Other apps (such as Showtimes, Eventful, WhosHere, and various travel apps) can grab this physical location information and use it to help you find things closer to you.

You can turn Location Services on or off by choosing Settings⇨General from the Home screen and then tapping the Off button for Location Services to turn it on, or the On button to turn it off.

After turning it off, your iPod touch prompts you to turn it back on if you run an app that makes use of Location Services (such as Maps).

To conserve battery power, turn off Location Services if you aren't using applications that make use of it.

Setting restrictions

If you need to, you can set restrictions that

- ✔ Prevent access to explicit music, podcasts, and videos according to ratings.
- ✔ Prevent the use of apps such as YouTube.
- ✔ Disallow in-app purchases.
- ✔ Stop any access to the iTunes Store or App Store.

Choose Settings⇨General from the Home screen and then tap Restrictions to see the Restrictions screen. Tap Enable Restrictions and then set up a restrictions passcode (which is separate from your Passcode Lock passcode). Enter a four-number passcode by touching numbers in the calculator-style keypad. If you change your mind, tap the Cancel button to cancel the operation. Then enter the same passcode number again to confirm the passcode, and the Restrictions are enabled and appear ready for you to change.

Set the restrictions you want by tapping each control's On switch to turn it off. By default, all controls are on, which means usage is allowed (not restricted). Turn off a control to restrict its use.

To turn off all restrictions, choose Settings⇨General⇨Restrictions and then enter the passcode. Tap Disable Restrictions and then reenter the passcode. Your iPod touch is now free. Be careful out there!

Part II
Filling Up Your Empty Cup

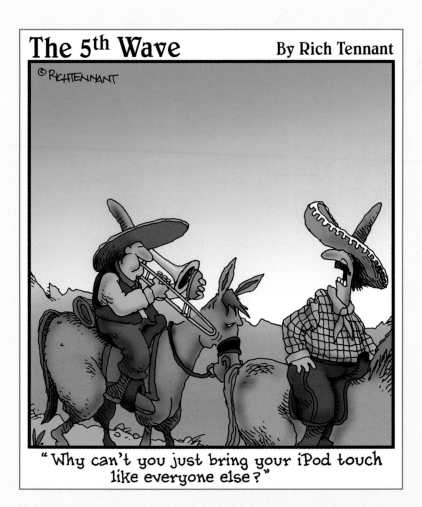

The 5th Wave

By Rich Tennant

"Why can't you just bring your iPod touch like everyone else?"

*T*his part shows you how to fill up your iPod touch with extreme content and killer apps.

First, in Chapter 4, you find out all about iTunes and how to set yourself up with an iTunes Store account. You're then given free reign to browse the store online from iTunes or browse for tunes and apps directly from your iPod touch. You also find out how to connect to a Wi-Fi network.

Next, in Chapter 5, I show you how to synchronize your iPod touch with your iTunes library, which you can fill up with songs from audio CDs and other content and apps from the iTunes Store. You can match your iPod touch library song for song with your iTunes library, or you can be more selective about what you copy to your iPod touch. You can also make sure your iPod touch downloads, including apps, are backed up in your iTunes library.

Then, in Chapter 6, I show you how to organize and synchronize your personal information with your iPod touch — your contacts, calendars, Web bookmarks, and e-mail accounts.

After all that, your iPod touch should be filled to the brim!

4

Exploring iTunes and the Online Store

In This Chapter

▶ Finding out all about iTunes

▶ Setting up an account with the iTunes Store

▶ Previewing and buying songs, TV shows, movies, and apps

▶ Choosing Wi-Fi to go online

▶ Downloading music, podcasts, and apps directly to your iPod touch

*1*f the iPod touch were a spaceship, iTunes would be the space station it docks with to get its supplies. iTunes is the central repository of all content and iPod touch apps, and it's the gateway to the online iTunes Store and App Store from your computer.

The iTunes Store offers millions of songs, with most songs available for download for 99 cents each and entire albums available for download at less than the list price of a CD. You can also buy audio books, TV episodes, and first-run movies. On top of that, iTunes offers tons of free content in the form of *podcasts,* which are similar to syndicated radio and TV shows. You can download podcasts into iTunes and play them at your convenience on your computer and on your iPod touch. iTunes even offers free lectures, language lessons, and audio books with educational content in its iTunes U section.

The iTunes Store includes the App Store, which offers free and commercial iPod touch applications by the tens of thousands. You can find apps in just about every category you can think of, including gaming, social networking, sports, business, and more. And after you've organized your content and apps in your iTunes library, you can put them on your iPod touch to carry around with you.

You can also download free or commercial content and apps directly from your iPod touch. The music and podcast sections of iTunes Store and the entire App Store are available right at your fingertips. You can download items and then synchronize them with your iTunes library.

This chapter gives you an overview of what you can do with iTunes, and it shows you how to sign in and take advantage of what the iTunes Store and App Store have to offer.

Discovering What You Can Do with iTunes

iTunes is the software that manages content on my iPod touch, all my other iPods, my iPhone, and even my Apple TV. Whether I buy content through my iPod touch, my iPhone, or my computer running iTunes, it all ends up in my iTunes library on my computer. I also bring content into iTunes from CDs and downloaded MP3 files. I then parcel the content out to various devices for playback.

All my content is stored in my main iTunes library on my computer, and backed up to another hard drive and to DVDs and CDs. You can manage all these activities with iTunes.

You can add videos to your iTunes library in a couple of ways: by choosing content from the iTunes Store (such as TV shows, feature-length high-definition movies, music videos, and even free movie trailers) or by downloading standard video files in the MPEG-4 format from other sources on the Internet. You can also create your own videos with a digital camcorder (or cameras built into computers, such as the iSight camera included with MacBooks and iMacs) and copy them to iTunes.

Although you can't use iTunes to transfer video content from a DVD, you can use other software to convert DVDs to digital video files, and you can transfer video content from older VHS players by using a digital video camcorder. Visit my Tony's Tips site at www.tonybove.com/tonytips for more details.

As if that weren't enough, iTunes gives you the power to organize content into playlists. A *playlist* is a list of the items that you want in the sequence that you want to play them. For example, you can make a playlist of love songs from different albums to play the next time you need a romantic mood, or you can compile a playlist of surf songs for a trip to the beach. You can even combine videos and music in a playlist.

If you organize songs into playlists in iTunes, you can then easily synchronize those playlists with your iPod touch to be more selective about the music you copy. See Chapter 5 for sync details. (Also, see my other book, *iPod & iTunes For Dummies,* to find out all about iTunes.)

What's that you say? You're still not satisfied with what iTunes can do for you? Well, iTunes also has a built-in equalizer with preset settings for all kinds of music and listening environments, with the added bonus of being able to customize and save your own personalized settings with each item of content.

You can run iTunes anytime (with or without your iPod touch attached to your computer) to build and manage your library. You don't have to connect your iPod touch until you're ready to sync it (as I describe in Chapter 5).

Browsing your iTunes library

The Mac and Windows versions of iTunes look nearly identical and offer the same functions and viewing options, including the *cover browser* (also known as Cover Flow). Figure 4-1 shows the iTunes window on the Mac with the cover browser open, displaying the cover art for albums.

iTunes offers a view of your library and your sources for content, as well as controls for organizing, importing, and playing content, as follows:

- **Source pane:** Displays the source of content, handily divided into the following sections:

  - *Library:* Includes your music, movies, TV shows, podcasts, audio books, applications and games, ringtones, and all available radio stations.

  - *Store:* Includes the iTunes Store, your shopping cart (if you turned on the Shopping Cart option in your Preferences, as described later in this chapter), and your Purchased list.

  - *Devices:* Includes audio CDs and any iPods, iPhones, and Apple TV devices (such as TB's Apple TV in Figure 4-1; TB being my initials) that are connected to your computer.

  - *Playlists:* Includes iTunes DJ and your playlists.

- **Cover browser:** Also called Cover Flow, the cover browser lets you flip through your cover art to choose songs. You can use the slider to move swiftly through your library, or you can click to the right or left of the cover in the foreground to move forward or backward in your library.

✔ **List pane:** Depending on the source that's selected in the Source pane, the List pane displays a list of items.

✔ **Player buttons — Forward/Next, Play/Pause, and Previous/Rewind:** Use these buttons to control the playback of content in iTunes.

✔ **Volume control:** You can change the volume level in iTunes by dragging the volume control slider in the upper-left section of the iTunes window to the right to increase the volume, or to the left to decrease it.

✔ **Status pane:** When content is playing, you can see the artist name, piece title (if known), and the elapsed time displayed in this pane.

✔ **View buttons:** The three buttons in the upper-right corner change your view of the List pane to show items in a list, show cover art thumbnail images in a grid, or show the cover browser.

✔ **Search field:** Type in this field to search your library. You can also use the Search field to peruse a playlist or to look within the iTunes Store.

✔ **Playlist buttons — Add, Shuffle, Repeat:** Use these buttons to add playlists and shuffle or repeat playback of playlists.

✔ **Show/Hide Artwork button:** Use this button to display or hide artwork associated with your music or videos (either your own or the artwork supplied by the iTunes Store).

✔ **Speakers pop-up menu:** Use this pop-up menu in the lower-right corner of the iTunes window to select a different speaker system than the computer's speakers. This pop-up menu appears only if you choose Preferences (from the iTunes menu on a Mac or the Edit menu in Windows), click the Devices tab, and turn on the Look for Remote Speakers Connected with AirTunes option. If iTunes locates remote speakers connected to an Airport Express or Apple TV using AirTunes (the technology for streaming music over a Wi-Fi or Ethernet local area network), the pop-up menu appears.

✔ **Genius button:** The Genius button, located in the lower-right corner of the iTunes window to the left of the Show/Hide Genius Sidebar button, generates a playlist of songs from your library that go great with the song you selected. The Genius button appears only when you've selected music, movies, TV shows, or a playlist. (See Chapter 7 for details about creating Genius playlists.)

✔ **Show/Hide Genius Sidebar button:** Use this button to display or hide the Genius sidebar. The Genius sidebar makes suggestions for what to get from the iTunes Store based on what you've selected.

✔ **Eject button:** This button appears next to the name of an audio CD or iPod touch in the Source pane to eject the CD or iPod touch. Clicking the Eject button for a CD physically ejects the CD so that it pops out. Clicking Eject for an iPod touch removes *(unmounts)* the iPod touch from the system so that you can disconnect it.

Source pane

Play/Pause

Rewind   Forward   ⌐ Volume control   Status pane

View buttons   Cover browser

Search field

Artwork
pane   Show/Hide Artwork   Speakers menu   List
pane

Add   Repeat   Genius button
Playlist   Shuffle   Show/Hide Genius Sidebar   Browse
Covers
Full-
screen

Figure 4-1: The iTunes window on a Mac with the cover browser open.

Setting up an iTunes Store account

One important task that you must do is set up your iTunes Store account. You can set it up in iTunes on your computer, or directly on your iPod touch (as I describe in "Shopping with Your iPod touch," later in this chapter). You need an account to purchase content or apps on your computer as well as to use the iTunes Store and App Store apps on your iPod touch. You can create as many accounts as you need — perhaps one for each family member. To create an iTunes Store account using iTunes on your computer, follow these steps:

1. **In iTunes, click the iTunes Store option in the Store section of the Source pane.**

   The iTunes Store home page appears, as shown in Figure 4-2, replacing the List pane.

2. **Click the Sign In button in the upper-right area of the window (refer to Figure 4-2) to either create an account or sign in to an existing account.**

   When you're logged in to an iTunes account, the account name appears in place of the Sign In button.

   After you click the Sign In button, iTunes displays the account sign-in dialog.

   TIP

   If you already set up an account with the iTunes Store with the MobileMe (formerly .Mac) service or with other Apple services (such as the Apple Developer Connection), you're halfway there. Type your ID and password and then click the Sign In button. Apple remembers the personal information that you put in previously, so you don't have to re-enter it every time you visit the iTunes Store. If you forgot your password, click the Forgot Password? button, and iTunes provides a dialog so that you can answer your test question. If you answer correctly, iTunes e-mails your password to you.

3. **Click the Create New Account button.**

   iTunes displays a new page that welcomes you to the iTunes Store.

4. **Click Continue on the iTunes Store welcome page.**

   After you click Continue, the terms of use appear with the option at the end to agree to the terms. If you don't select the option to agree, the iTunes continues to display the terms until you agree or click Cancel.

5. **Select the I Have Read and Agree to the iTunes Terms and Conditions option to agree with the legal terms. Then click Continue.**

   iTunes displays the next page of the setup procedure.

6. **Fill in your personal account information.**

   You need to enter your e-mail address, password, test question and answer (in case you forget your password), birthdate, and privacy options. *Don't forget your password* — you need it to access the store from your iPod touch.

7. **Click the Continue button to go to the next page of the account setup procedure and then enter your credit card information.**

   The entire procedure is secure, so you don't have to worry. The iTunes Store keeps your personal information (including your credit card information) on file, and you don't have to type it again.

8. Click Continue to finish the procedure.

The account setup finishes and returns you to the iTunes Store home page. You can now use the iTunes Store to purchase and download content to play in iTunes and use on any iPod, iPhone, or Apple TV.

Back

Forward | Home Page

Sign In button

Figure 4-2: The iTunes Store home page.

Shopping at the iTunes Store

If you have an iTunes Store account set up (see the previous section), you can buy and download content immediately, including movies for rent. I don't know of a faster way to purchase or rent content from the comfort of your home.

If you already have your iTunes program open, click iTunes Store in the Store section of the Source pane. The iTunes Store home page opens (refer to Figure 4-2).

Cruising in the multimedia mall

The iTunes Store home page is loaded with specials and advertisements to peruse. To look at music in more depth, choose Music from the iTunes Store panel at the top left of the home page (next to the New and Noteworthy panel — refer to Figure 4-2). iTunes displays more panels of advertisements and specials for music lovers. You can then choose a genre from the Genres pop-up menu on the iTunes Store panel to see only those specials and ads for a particular genre.

The iTunes Store also provides buttons on a gray bar just above the advertised content in the List pane (refer to Figure 4-2). The left and right triangle buttons work just like the Back and Forward buttons of a Web browser, moving back a page or forward a page, respectively. The button with the Home icon takes you to the iTunes Store home page.

After selecting an advertisement for an album, for example, the album's page appears with a description and other links, as shown in Figure 4-3. The iTunes Store uses the iTunes List pane to display the contents of the album.

Figure 4-3: You can view an album's songs in the iTunes Store.

You can preview any song in the iTunes Store for up to 30 seconds. Some movies offer one-minute previews and movie trailers you can view for free, and TV shows and audio books can offer up to 90 seconds. To preview a song, TV show, movie, or music video, click the title in the list and then click the Play button (or press the spacebar).

Videos play in the Artwork pane in the lower-left corner of the iTunes window, as shown in Figure 4-4. If the Artwork pane isn't visible, click the Show/Hide Artwork button to display it. Click the iTunes player buttons to control playback, and use the iTunes volume slider to control the volume.

Figure 4-4: You can even preview a TV episode.

Buying and downloading items

The iTunes Store thoughtfully gives you two different methods for purchasing and downloading items, and you're free to switch between methods at your leisure. The two methods are

✔ **1-Click:** 1-Click shopping is the default method. Whenever you're ready, you can purchase a song or any other item and download it to your computer. All you need to do is click the Buy button, whether the item is a song, an album, a TV show episode, or an audio book.

For example, if you select a song in the List pane, click the Buy Song button in the far-right column for the song (refer to Figure 4-3). (You might have to scroll your iTunes Store window to see the far-right column.) When you select a TV show episode, click the Buy Episode button in the far-right column (refer to Figure 4-4). You can also click the Buy Album button in an album advertisement.

✔ **Shopping Cart:** Alternatively, you can gather your selections in a virtual shopping cart first to see your choices and decide whether to purchase them before downloading them all at once. With the shopping cart, the iTunes Store remembers your selections, allowing you to browse the iTunes Store at different times and add to your total without making any purchases final. You can also remove items from the cart at any time. When you're ready to buy, you can purchase and download the items in your cart in one fell swoop.

To change your shopping method, choose iTunes⇨Preferences on the Mac or Edit⇨Preferences in Windows. In the Preferences window, click the Store button. Select the Shopping Cart option.

Wait — before you close the Store Preferences window and run off to buy stuff, take note of some cool features: This window lets you set the option to automatically check for available downloads from the iTunes Store — such as downloads that were not completed — and new episodes for a podcast subscription. You can even set options to automatically download pre-purchased or Season Pass content as well as missing album artwork.

After switching to the Shopping Cart method and closing the Store Preferences window, the Buy button changes to an Add button — as in Add Song, Add Album, Add Episode, and so on. After adding items, you can view the selections in your shopping cart by going to the Source pane and selecting the Shopping Cart option underneath the iTunes Store option in the Store section. (Refer to Figure 4-1.)

The shopping cart appears in the List view with your selections listed, and recommendations from the iTunes Store appear along the top of the window. Albums appear with a triangle next to their names, which you can click to open in order to see the album's songs. When you're ready to purchase everything in your shopping cart, click the BUY NOW button in the lower-right corner of the Shopping Cart view to close the sale and download all the items at once. Alternatively, you can click the Buy (for an album) or Buy Song buttons for each item that you want to purchase.

The iTunes Store may prompt you to log in to your account after you click the Buy button (unless you just recently logged in). It then displays a warning dialog to make sure that you want to buy the item (or items, if you're using a shopping cart), and you can then go through with it by clicking the Buy button, or cancel. After you click the Buy button, iTunes downloads the item or items and, after downloading, they appear in your iTunes library. The iTunes Store keeps track of your purchases over a 24-hour period and charges you for a total sum rather than for each single purchase.

To delete items from your shopping cart, select them and press Delete/Backspace. A warning appears, asking whether you're sure that you want to remove the selected items. Click Yes to go ahead and remove the selections from your shopping cart.

You can see the list of all the items that you purchased (no matter which shopping method you used at the time) by selecting the Purchased playlist under the iTunes Store option in the Source pane. The List view and Browse view change to show the items you purchased.

If you use more than one computer to access your iTunes Store account, you can set the preferences for each computer differently and still use the same account. For example, your home computer might have a faster connection than your laptop on a remote connection, so you can set your iTunes preferences accordingly: The home computer could be set to 1-Click, and the laptop could be set to shopping cart.

Each time you buy content, you get an e-mail from the iTunes Store with the purchase information. It's nice to know right away what you bought.

Appearing at the App Store

You can get loads of free and commercial apps that run on your iPod touch just like the built-in apps such as Map and Weather. (To no one's big surprise, many of the apps are games.) To find thousands of apps, click App Store in the iTunes Store panel on the iTunes Store home page (refer to Figure 4-2). The App Store page appears, as shown in Figure 4-5.

Click an app's icon to go to the information page for that app, which may also contain reviews and a slideshow depicting the app in all its glory. The information page offers the Buy App button (to purchase and download a commercial app), or the Get App button (to download a free app). Click the Buy App or Get App button to download the app to your iTunes library.

Downloaded apps appear in the Applications section of your iTunes library (refer to Figure 4-1) — click Applications in the Library section of the Source pane to see their icons. If you don't see Applications in the Source pane, choose iTunes➪Preferences (Mac) or Edit➪Preferences (Windows), click the General tab at the top of the Preferences window, select the Applications option from the list of options for the Show heading, and click OK. The Applications option then appears in the Source pane in the Library section.

Figure 4-5: iPod touch apps in the App Store section of the iTunes Store.

When an app you downloaded is updated, iTunes informs you — the message Update Available appears at the bottom of the Applications section with an arrow link that takes you to the My Apps Update page in the iTunes Store, with icons of the apps to update. Click the Get Update button next to each app to download the update, which automatically replaces the previous version of the app.

Going Online with Your iPod touch

To use the iTunes Store and App Store on your iPod touch, you must first join a Wi-Fi network that's connected to the Internet. The iPod touch can join Wi-Fi networks at home, at work, or at Wi-Fi hotspots around the world. Although some public Wi-Fi networks are free, others require logging in first, and still others require logging in and supplying a credit card number. Still others are detected but locked — if you select a locked network, a dialog appears asking for a password.

If you don't have Wi-Fi at home but you do have a broadband Internet connection (such as cable or DSL), I recommend buying an AirPort Express or AirPort Extreme, available in the Apple Store — you can then connect your Internet connection to the AirPort to extend Internet access over Wi-Fi. AirPort Express is powerful enough to run a home Wi-Fi network yet portable enough to take on the road and use in hotel rooms that offer Internet connections, and it even plays music from your iTunes library through speakers connected to it. AirPort Extreme lets up to 50 users connect to Wi-Fi at once — perfect for a large family or small business. You can give your network a unique name, which appears in the list of networks on your iPod touch when your iPod touch is in range of it.

Turning Wi-Fi on or off

To turn Wi-Fi on, choose Settings⇨Wi-Fi from the Home screen to display the Wi-Fi Networks screen, and tap the Off button for the Wi-Fi setting to turn it on (tap it again to turn it off).

When Wi-Fi is turned on, your iPod touch detects and automatically acquires a Wi-Fi signal you've used before, or it can detect one or more signals in the area and present them in a list for you to choose. The list of available Wi-Fi networks appears below the Wi-Fi setting, as shown in Figure 4-6.

If your iPod touch isn't already connected to Wi-Fi, it's set by default to look for networks and ask whether you want to join them whenever you use something that requires the network (such as Safari, Weather, YouTube, Mail, and so on). You can stop your iPod touch from looking and asking: Scroll down to the end of the list of Wi-Fi networks on the Wi-Fi Networks screen and then tap the On button for the Ask to Join Networks option to turn it off. You can still join networks manually, but you won't be interrupted with requests to join networks.

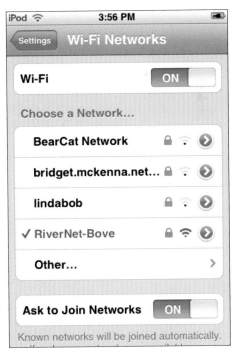

Figure 4-6: Enable Wi-Fi and then choose a Wi-Fi network.

Choosing a Wi-Fi network

You can scroll the list of networks in the Wi-Fi Networks screen to choose one. (Refer to Figure 4-6.) You can scroll quickly by flicking your finger or scroll slowly by dragging up or down, but however you scroll, you choose a Wi-Fi network by tapping its name. Networks are named by their administrators. (If you set up your own home Wi-Fi, you get to name yours whatever you want.)

When connected to a Wi-Fi network, your iPod touch displays the Wi-Fi icon in the status bar at the top of the display, which also indicates the connection strength — the more bars you see, the stronger the connection.

If a Lock icon appears next to the Wi-Fi network name (refer to Figure 4-6), it means the network is locked and you need a password. When you select a locked network, the iPod touch displays an Enter Password screen and the onscreen keyboard. Tap out the password using the keyboard. (For details on how to use the onscreen keyboard, see Chapter 2.) Tap Join to join the network or tap Cancel in the upper-right corner to cancel joining.

To join a Wi-Fi network that requires either a credit card or an account for you to log in, select the network and then use Safari to open the network's Web page. (For more on using Safari, see Chapter 10.) The first Web page you see is typically the log-in page for the service (for example, a commercial Wi-Fi service or a hotel service).

Your iPod touch remembers your Wi-Fi connections and automatically uses one when it detects it within your range. If you've used multiple Wi-Fi networks in the same location, it picks the last one you used.

You can also *forget* a network — such as a paid or closed Wi-Fi service that somehow got hold of your iPod touch and won't let you move on to other Web pages without typing a password. See Chapter 15 for the details about how to forget a network.

Shopping with Your iPod touch

The music, movies, TV shows, music videos, podcasts, and audiobooks in the iTunes store as well as the entire App Store, are available right at your fingertips on your iPod touch. You can search for, browse, and preview content; make purchases; and download content directly to your iPod touch.

Whatever you buy on your iPod touch is automatically copied to your iTunes library the next time you synchronize it with your computer, as I describe in Chapter 5.

Be sure to set up an iTunes Store account first if you don't already have one, as I describe earlier in this chapter — and you'll need to remember your password. To download content and apps directly to your iPod touch, you can set up your iPod touch with iTunes, which basically means signing in to your iTunes Store account in iTunes on your computer, and then syncing your iPod touch to iTunes as I describe in Chapter 5. After doing that once, you shouldn't have to bother with it again, and you'll be able to download items from the iTunes Store and App Store on your iPod touch from then on. All you need to do is enter the password for your iTunes Store account when prompted.

You can also set up one or more iTunes Store accounts directly from your iPod touch: choose Settings➪Store from the Home screen and then tap Create New Account. Confirm your country or region and touch Next. Tap Agree to the terms of service, and then enter the information on the New Account screen with the onscreen keyboard. (The information you need to supply is the same as shown in "Setting up an iTunes Store account," earlier in this chapter.) Tap Next to continue through the setup screens to finish setting up your account.

To sign into an existing account, choose Settings➪Store and then tap Sign In. You can then type in your account name and password. You can also view your account information at any time by choosing Settings➪Store and tapping View Account.

Browsing and downloading content

To go to the iTunes Store on an iPod touch, tap the iTunes icon on the Home screen. The store screen appears with Music, Videos, Podcast, Search, and More icons along the bottom. Here's the lowdown on the icons.

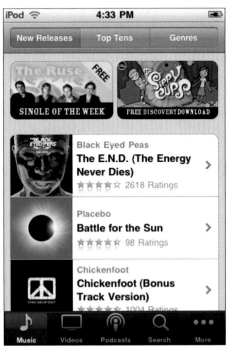

Figure 4-7: You can browse the iTunes Store on an iPod touch.

✔ **Tap the Music icon** to see Music items, new releases, and store recommendations, as shown in Figure 4-7. The screen displays New Releases, Top Tens, and Genres buttons along the top. To search through genres, tap the Genres button and choose a genre. Tap the Top Tens button to see a list of the top ten choices in different genres. Choose iTunes in the Top Tens list to see the top ten songs throughout the iTunes Store. Tap Music in the top-left corner to return to the previous Music screen.

✔ **Tap the Videos icon** and the screen displays Movies, TV Shows, and Music Videos buttons along the top. Tap Movies to see new movie releases; TV Shows to see new and noteworthy TV shows; or Music Videos to see the hottest music videos in the iTunes Store. Tap Videos in the top-left corner to return to the previous Videos screen.

✔ **Tap the Podcasts icon** and the screen displays What's Hot, Top Tens, and Categories buttons along the top. Tap What's Hot to see the most popular podcasts; Categories to view categories of podcasts; or Top Tens to see the top ten in each category. Tap Podcasts in the top-left corner to return to the previous Podcasts screen.

✔ **Tap the Search icon** to search the store and then tap the entry field to bring up the onscreen keyboard. Type the search term and tap the Search button to search the store.

✔ **Tap the More icon** and then either select Audiobooks to buy audio books, iTunes U to download learning content, Downloads to see the progress of your downloads from the store, or Redeem to redeem gift certificates.

If this is your first time to the store on your iPod touch, the Music section appears with New Releases in a scrollable list. Tap any song to hear a preview. To buy and download a song, tap the button with the price tag. Enter your password and tap OK.

You can similarly preview and buy videos — tap the video, then tap the Preview button to see a preview, and tap the Buy (with price tag) button to buy it and download it.

After selecting a podcast, a list of episodes appears. Tap the Free button (or Buy button for paid podcasts) next to an episode, enter your password, and then tap OK to start downloading the podcast episode.

Purchased and downloaded items are added to a Purchased playlist on your iPod touch, and they're included in your Purchased playlist in iTunes as well as in a special Purchased on *YourDeviceName* playlist. iTunes automatically syncs items downloaded on your iPod touch to your iTunes library when you connect it to your computer so that you have a backup if you delete them from the iPod touch.

Some albums offer bonus content, such as liner notes, which are downloaded to your iTunes library on your computer, but not to your iPod touch. Also note that an alert appears on your iPod touch if you've previously purchased one or more songs from an album. Tap Buy if you want to purchase the entire album, or tap Cancel if you want to buy the remaining songs on the album individually.

If you lose your network connection or turn off your iPod touch while down-loading, the download pauses and then resumes when you reestablish Wi-Fi. If you go back to your computer, iTunes can complete the download opera-tion to your iTunes library. To make sure you received all your downloads from purchases on your iPod touch, use iTunes on your computer and choose Store⇒Check for Available Downloads.

Browsing and downloading apps

To use the App Store, tap the App Store icon on the Home screen. The Store screen appears with Featured, Categories, Top 25, Search, and More icons along the bottom. The following list tells you what's what when it comes to the icons:

✓ **Tap the Featured icon** and then tap the What's Hot button at the top to see the most popu-lar apps based on downloads, or tap the New button to see featured new apps, as shown in Figure 4-8.

✓ To browse by category, **tap the Categories icon** in the bottom menu and then tap a category, such as Games, to see a list of all games by popularity.

✓ **Tap the Top 25 icon** in the bottom menu and then tap Top Paid to see the top 25 paid apps by popularity, or tap Top Free to see the top 25 free apps.

✓ **Tap the Search icon** to search the store, and tap the entry field to bring up the onscreen keyboard. Type the search term and tap Search to search the store. Suggestions pop up right away; for example, if you search for "Tony" in the App Store, my app, Tony's Tips for iPhone Users Manual, appears in the list of suggestions.

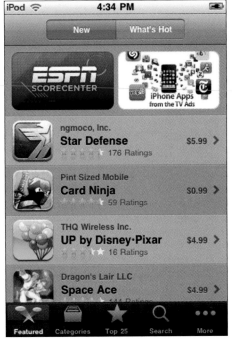

Figure 4-8: Browsing the new featured apps in the App Store on an iPod touch.

✓ **Tap the More icon** to select Redeem to redeem gift certificates, or Updates to . . . er, I explain that one in the next section.

To view information and to purchase and download an app, tap the app in the list that appears after tapping the Featured, Categories, Top 25, or Search icon. You can then scroll the display to see more information about the app.

To download an app, tap the Price button (for a paid app) or Free button (for a free app). The Price or Free button changes to the Install button. Tap Install and then enter your password and tap OK.

The iPod touch displays the Home screen with the icon for the new app as it loads. As soon as the Loading message is replaced by the name of the app, the icon is ready to be tapped.

Updating apps you've downloaded

The App Store on your iPod touch notifies you if any of your apps have been updated — a number appears in the App Store icon. You should update an app when an update is available because updates fix bugs and introduce new features you may want.

Tap the More icon at the bottom-right corner of the App Store screen and then tap Updates to see the list of updated apps. To update an app, tap the app in the list to see the app's information screen and then tap the Update button. The Update button changes to the Install button. Tap Install and then enter your password and tap OK.

The update replaces the previous version of the app as it loads into your iPod touch. As soon as the Loading message is replaced by the name of the app, the icon is ready to be tapped.

Now you're ready to sync with your iTunes library the apps and content you downloaded into your iPod touch — sink gently into the next chapter.

Into the Sync with iTunes

In This Chapter

▶ Synchronizing your iPod touch with your iTunes Store account

▶ Synchronizing your iTunes library with your iPod touch

▶ Copying songs and videos directly to, or deleting them from, your iPod touch

Synchronizing your iPod touch with iTunes means keeping it up-to-date with your iTunes library — matching it song for song, movie for movie, and so on. The sync operation also keeps both your iPod touch and your computer up-to-date with your iTunes Store account information as well as with items downloaded from the iTunes Store or App Store directly to your iPod touch.

If you make changes in iTunes after syncing the iPod touch, those changes are automatically made in the iPod touch when you sync again. Your iPod touch mirrors as much of the content of your iTunes library as will fit, making assumptions if the entire library won't fit.

The full, everything-but-the-kitchen-sync approach works well if your combined iTunes library and photo library are small enough to fit in their entirety on your iPod touch. For example, if your iTunes and photo libraries combined are less than 29GB and you have a 32GB iPod touch, sync everything. (You can see the size of your iTunes library in GB, or *gigabytes,* at the bottom of the iTunes window in the center.) Syncing everything copies your entire library, and it's just as fast as copying individual items (if not faster) because you don't have to select the items to copy.

If your libraries are larger than your iPod touch, you can make decisions about which parts to sync. You can select options to synchronize music, TV shows, movies, and so on. For example, you can copy all your songs and audio books, but only some of your TV shows, none of your movies, and only the podcasts you haven't heard yet.

This chapter also describes how to copy songs, videos, podcasts, and audio books directly to your iPod touch using the manual method. You can even combine automatic syncing with manual methods to build your iPod touch library as you see fit.

Syncing with Your iTunes Library and Account

It's easy to sync your iPod touch with your computer so you can copy content and apps to the iPod touch from your iTunes library. It's also necessary for copying any iPod touch purchases or downloads back to your computer for safekeeping. Syncing also makes sure that your iPod touch is set with your iTunes Store account information if you haven't set the account up by hand with your iPod touch (as I describe in Chapter 4.) To make sure your iPod touch is set with your iTunes Store account information, sign in first to the iTunes Store, and then sync your iPod touch.

After syncing your iPod touch, iTunes copies anything you downloaded to your iPod touch back to your iTunes library — that way you don't lose any media if, heaven forbid, something happens to your iPod touch.

Follow these steps to sync your iPod touch with iTunes:

1. **With iTunes running, visit the iTunes Store and sign in to your account.**

   You don't have to buy anything; just signing into the store provides all the info you need to sync your iPod touch with the iTunes Store account. (If you haven't set up your iTunes Store account yet, flip back to Chapter 4, do the deed, and then sign in by clicking the Sign In button in the upper-right area of the iTunes window.) When you're signed in to an iTunes Store account, the account name appears in place of the Sign In button.

2. **Connect the iPod touch and select its name when it appears in the Devices section of the Source pane.**

   iTunes displays the iPod touch sync options to the right of the Source pane, with the Summary page (under the Summary tab) open. The Summary page shows how much space on the device is occupied by content and how much is still free. (See Figure 5-1.)

Figure 5-1: The iPod touch Summary page in iTunes offers sync options.

3. **If the iPod touch isn't automatically synchronizing, click the Sync button in the bottom-right corner to synchronize it.**

   You can select the content you want to synchronize, as I describe later in this chapter, or sync with whatever selections you've already made and change them later when you re-sync.

   After clicking the Sync button, the iTunes Status pane tells you that iTunes is syncing the iPod touch.

4. **Wait for the synchronization to finish and then click the Eject button next to the iPod touch name in the Source pane.**

   You should always wait until the iTunes Status pane (at the top) displays that the synchronization is complete.

5. **Disconnect your iPod touch from your computer.**

   That's it. Your iPod touch is now synchronized.

Copying Everything

After connecting the iPod touch to iTunes, you can copy everything at once by following Steps 2–5 in the previous section (refer to Figure 5-1). Most likely your iPod touch is already set to automatically synchronize with iTunes after connecting it. If you haven't made any sync selections, the default is to copy everything in your iTunes library to your iPod touch.

Photos you've organized in an iPhoto library (on a Mac) or in a program (such as Adobe Photoshop Album in Windows) are also copied over. See Chapter 9 for details.

If your iTunes library is too large to fit on your iPod touch, iTunes decides which songs and albums to include by using the ratings that you set for each song. (To find out how to set ratings, see Chapter 15.) If your iPod touch already has photos on it, iTunes asks whether you want to delete them to gain more space. After clicking Yes or No, iTunes tries its best to fit everything. If it has to cut something, though, it skips copying new photos and displays the message Some photos were not copied.

If you're still short of space even after skipping photos, iTunes displays a warning about the lack of free space, and it asks whether you want to disable podcast synchronization and let iTunes create a selection of songs in a playlist based on ratings and playback counts in iTunes. (A *playlist* is a list of the items that you want in the sequence that you want to play them — you can use playlists to organize your music playback experience.)

✔ **If you click Yes,** iTunes creates a new playlist (titled "*Your device name* Selection," as in "My iPod touch Selection") and displays a message telling you so. Click OK, and iTunes synchronizes your iPod touch using the new playlist. iTunes also sets your iPod touch to synchronize music automatically by playlist, as I describe in the next section.

✔ **If you click No,** iTunes updates automatically until it fills your iPod touch without creating the playlist.

From that point on, your iPod touch synchronizes with your iTunes library automatically, right after you connect it to your computer. If you add or delete content in your iTunes library, that content is added or deleted in the iPod touch when you sync again.

By the way, to find out more about creating playlists, consult *iPod & iTunes For Dummies* by yours truly (Wiley Publishing, Inc.).

During the synchronization process, iTunes also performs a backup of the sync settings and other settings for your iPod touch from the last time when you synchronized it.

To prevent an iPod touch from automatically synchronizing, press ⌘-Option (Mac) or Ctrl-Alt (Windows) while you connect the device, and then keep pressing until the iPod touch name appears in the iTunes Source pane. You can then change the iPod touch sync setting to manually manage music and videos, as I describe later in this chapter.

If you connect an iPod touch previously linked to another computer to *your* computer, iTunes displays a message warning you that clicking Yes replaces the iPod touch content with the content from your computer's library. If you don't want to change the iPod's content, click No. If you click Yes, iTunes erases the iPod touch and synchronizes it with your computer's library. To avoid this warning, first set the iPod touch sync settings to manually manage music and videos.

Choosing What to Sync

If you have a massive music library, one that would never fit on even the most capacious of iPod touches, you can go the selective route, choosing which content to automatically sync with your iTunes library. By synchronizing selectively, you can still make your iPod touch match at least a subset of your iTunes library. If you make changes to that subset in iTunes, those changes are automatically made in the device when you synchronize again.

Syncing everything but the kitchen

You can decide which items you *don't* want to synchronize and simply not include them by first *deselecting* them one by one in your iTunes library. (If you have a large iTunes library, this may take some time — you may find it easier to synchronize by playlists, as I show you later in this section.)

By default, all content items are selected — a check mark appears in the check box next to the item. To deselect an item in your iTunes library, click the check box next to the item so that the check mark disappears. To reselect an item, just click the check box again.

You can quickly select (or deselect) an entire album by showing the Browser (choose View➪Show Browser) and choosing the album in the far-right column of the Browser view, and then pressing ⌘ (Mac) or Ctrl (Windows) while selecting (or deselecting) a single song in the album in the List view below the Browser columns.

After you deselect the items you don't want to transfer, connect your iPod touch to your computer and select its name when it appears in the Devices section of the Source pane (refer to Figure 5-1). Then select the Sync Only Checked Songs and Videos option. Click Apply and continue with Steps 3–5 in the earlier section, "Syncing with Your iTunes Store Account."

iTunes restarts synchronization and deletes from the iPod touch any items in the library that are deselected, to save space, before adding back in the items in the iTunes library that are selected. That means the items you deselected are now *gone* from your iPod touch — replaced by whatever items were selected. Of course, the items are still in your iTunes library.

Getting picky about playlists

You can include just the items that are defined in playlists, including Genius playlists. Syncing by playlist is a great way of syncing vast amounts of music without syncing the entire library.

To find out more about creating smart and Genius playlists, consult *iPod & iTunes For Dummies* by yours truly.

For example, you can create four playlists that contain all essential rock, folk, blues, and jazz albums, and then select all four, or just one, two, or three of these playlists to synchronize with your iPod touch.

Before using this option, create the playlists in iTunes that you want to copy to your iPod touch. Connect your iPod touch to your computer, and select its name when it appears in the Devices section of the Source pane (refer to Figure 5-1). Then click the Music tab of the sync options. (You may have to click Apply first to apply the changes you made to other sync options pages.) The Music sync options page appears, as shown in Figure 5-2.

To select all the music and audio books in your library, select the Sync Music option and then select the All Songs and Playlists option on the Music sync options page.

To choose playlists, select the Sync Music and the Selected Playlists options, and from the list box, select each playlist that you want to synchronize with the iPod touch. You can scroll the list box to see all your playlists. In Figure 5-2, I chose the My Top Rated playlist.

Finally, click the Apply button to apply changes, and click the Sync button if synchronization hasn't already started automatically.

iTunes copies only the music and audio books in these playlists. If you also select the Include Music Videos option on the Music sync options page (as I do in Figure 5-2), iTunes includes music videos listed in the playlists. You can also select the Include Voice Memos option to sync your voice memos from the Voice Memo app with your iTunes library. (See Chapter 13 for details on using voice memo)

If you select the Sync Only Checked Songs and Videos option on the Summary page of the iPod touch sync options (refer to Figure 5-1), only selected items are copied. iTunes ignores items that are not selected, even if they're listed in the chosen playlists for synchronization.

Figure 5-2: Synchronize your iPod with only selected playlists.

Picking and choosing podcast episodes

You can get picky about which podcast episodes should be copied over during synchronization. The Podcasts tab of the sync pages for the iPod touch gives you options for choosing podcast episodes to include.

Connect your iPod touch to your computer, and select its name when it appears in the Devices section of the Source pane (refer to Figure 5-1). Then click the Podcasts tab. The Podcasts sync options page appears, as shown in Figure 5-3.

The Podcast sync options let you choose unplayed or recently added episodes. Select the Sync _____ Episodes Of check box and choose a modifier from the pop-up menu, such as All Unplayed episodes (as shown in Figure 5-3). You can also choose to sync episodes from all or just selected podcasts. For example, in Figure 5-3, I'm synchronizing all unplayed episodes of the selected podcasts.

Finally, click the Apply button to apply changes and click the Sync button if synchronization hasn't already started automatically.

Choosing movies and TV shows

Movies and TV shows take up a lot of space, so if you limit the movies and TV episodes you synchronize with your iPod touch, you gain extra space for more music, audio books, podcasts, and photos.

To get choosy about movies, connect your iPod touch to your computer and select its name when it appears in the Devices section of the Source pane (refer to Figure 5-1). Then click the Movies tab of the sync options. The Movies sync options page appears, as shown in Figure 5-4.

Select the Sync Movies check box (as shown in Figure 5-4). You can then choose to sync all movies, unwatched movies, recently added movies, or specific movies (as I do in Figure 5-4).

To pick only the TV episodes you want, click the TV Shows tab of the sync options. (You may have to click the Apply button first, to apply the changes you made to other sync options pages.) The TV Shows sync options page appears, as shown in Figure 5-5.

Select the Sync _____ Episodes Of option (as shown in Figure 5-5). You can then use the pop-up menu to choose All Unwatched episodes, as I do in Figure 5-5, or recently added episodes. You can also choose to sync all TV shows or only selected shows. For example, in Figure 5-5, I'm copying all unwatched episodes of *Star Trek: The Original Series* but no other TV shows.

Finally, click the Apply button to apply changes, and click the Sync button if synchronization hasn't already started automatically.

To find out about converting videos for use in iTunes and the iPod touch, visit my online tips at www.tonybove.com/tonytips.

Figure 5-3: Synchronize your iPod touch with all episodes of selected podcasts.

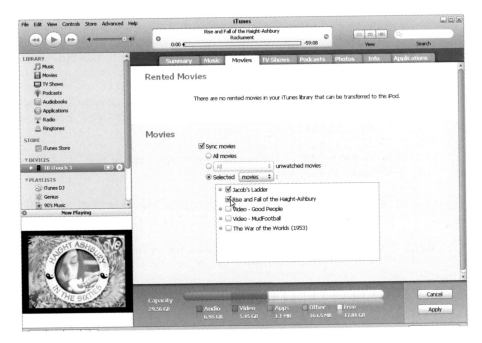

Figure 5-4: Synchronize your iPod with the selected movies only.

Figure 5-5: Synchronize your iPod touch with only selected TV show episodes.

Manually Managing Music and Videos

If your entire library is too big for your iPod touch, you may want to copy individual items directly. By setting your iPod touch to manually manage music and videos, you can add content to your iPod touch directly via iTunes, and you can delete content as well. You can even copy some songs or videos from another computer's iTunes library without deleting any content from your iPod touch.

To set your iPod touch to manually manage music and videos, first connect your iPod touch to your computer. Then follow these steps:

1. **Select the iPod touch name in the Devices section of the iTunes Source pane.**

   After selecting the name, the Summary page appears, displaying the iPod touch sync options (see Figure 5-6).

2. **Select the Manually Manage Music and Videos option, as shown in Figure 5-6.**

   iTunes displays a message warning you that disabling automatic synchronization requires manually ejecting the iPod touch before each disconnect.

Figure 5-6: Set your iPod touch to manually manage music and videos.

3. Click OK for the warning and click the Apply button to apply the change.

Don't disconnect your iPod touch while managing music and videos manually. You have to eject it first, as spelled out in the next section. If you don't, you may find that it doesn't work properly and needs to be restored, as I describe in Chapter 14.

That album is just a drag

You can now select and drag music and video — songs, albums, audio books, music videos, movies, and TV shows — to your iPod touch name in the Source pane. You can drag the media from its section in the iTunes library or from an existing playlist or drag an entire playlist. To do so, follow these steps:

1. In the iTunes Source pane, select the source of your media.

You might select Music in the Library section, for instance, or a playlist in the library.

You can select music in your library using List, Grid, or Cover Flow view (see Chapter 4 for browsing details), or select songs in a playlist.

2. **Drag items (such as an album) directly from your iTunes library or play-list over the iPod touch name in the Devices section of the Source pane.**

   You can drag an entire album from Cover Flow view, as I show in Figure 5-7, or from List or Grid view. When you drag an album cover or album title, all the songs in the album are copied. If you drag a playlist name from the Source pane to the iPod touch name, all the songs associated with the playlist copy along with the playlist itself.

Figure 5-7: Copy an album directly from the iTunes library to an iPod touch. (Mine is called Mojo iTouch.)

3. **Wait for the copying to finish and then click the Eject button next to the iPod touch name in the Source pane to eject the iPod touch.**

   Always wait until the iTunes Status pane (at the top) tells you that the copying is completed.

4. **Disconnect your iPod touch from your computer.**

Delete to make room for more

When you manually manage music and videos, you can also delete content from the iPod touch. Set the option to manually manage music and videos (if it isn't set that way already) and then follow these steps:

1. **In the Source pane, click the triangle to the left of the iPod touch name to expand its library.**

   The iPod touch library appears in the Source pane with Music, Movies, TV Shows, and other sections, followed by playlists. The library is indented underneath the iPod touch name.

2. **Click any content type in the iPod touch library to see the items.**

   The content items appear in the iTunes List pane to the right of the Source pane.

3. **Select an item and press Delete/Backspace or choose Edit⇨Delete.**

   iTunes displays a warning to make sure you want to do this; click OK to go ahead or Cancel to stop. If you want to delete a playlist, select the playlist underneath the iPod touch name in the Source pane and then press Delete or choose Edit⇨Delete.

Like in the iTunes library, if you delete a playlist, the songs listed in the play-list aren't deleted. They're still on your iPod touch unless you delete the songs directly from the iPod touch library.

Autofill it up

You can also automatically fill your iPod touch while managing music and videos manually: Autofill randomly picks songs from your entire iTunes library or from a playlist you select in the iTunes Source pane.

Set the option to manually manage music and videos (if it isn't set that way already). Then follow these steps:

1. **In the Source pane, click the triangle to the left of the iPod touch name to expand its library.**

   The iPod touch library appears in the Source pane.

2. **Select Music under the iPod touch name in the Devices section of the Source pane.**

   The music on your iPod touch appears in the List pane, along with the Autofill pane along the bottom, as shown in Figure 5-8.

3. **Choose your source of music in the Autofill From pop-up menu.**

   Choose either a playlist, as I did in Figure 5-8 (Purchased Music), or Music for the entire music library. If you choose a playlist, Autofill uses only the playlist as the source to pick random songs. After choosing your source of music, iTunes creates a playlist and displays it in the List pane.

4. **(Optional) Click the Settings button to set options and then click OK.**

Figure 5-8: Autofill your iPod touch from an iTunes playlist.

After you click the Settings button, the Autofill Settings dialog appears. You can choose to replace all the songs on the iPod touch, to pick songs randomly, and to pick only the best songs (if choosing randomly). If you don't select to replace all songs, iTunes adds the songs without replacing existing songs. Click OK to close the Autofill Settings dialog.

5. **Click the Autofill button to start copying songs.**

   iTunes copies the contents of the Autofill playlist to your iPod touch.

6. **Wait for the copy operation to finish and then click the Eject button.**

   Always wait until the iTunes Status pane (at the top) tells you that the copying is finished.

> **TIP**
> You can click the Autofill button over and over to create different random playlists. When you get one you like, select all its contents and choose File⇨New Playlist From Selection to create a new playlist that contains the songs generated by Autofill. The next time you connect your iPod touch, select this new playlist from the Autofill From pop-up menu and then click the Autofill button to load the music from the playlist to your iPod touch.

Syncing Your Day in the Life

In This Chapter

▶ Synchronizing e-mail, calendars, contacts, and bookmarks

▶ Using MobileMe to sync over the Internet

▶ Setting up e-mail accounts on your iPod touch

Your iPod touch can take care of all aspects of your digital life: It can send and receive e-mail, keep track of your calendar and notes, sort your contacts, and save bookmarks to all your favorite Web sites as you browse them.

If you're a road warrior, you may want to fill up your iPod touch with your personal information. You can then go out into the world, conquer it, and bring back new or edited contacts, new events, and new Web site bookmarks, which you can then synchronize back with your computer.

Apps to Organize Your Life

Where do I start? First off, your iPod touch has no problem sending and receiving e-mail using the Mail application (as I describe in Chapter 11). It also offers the Contacts app to store contact info, the Calendar app to store events (see Chapter 13), the Notes app to take notes (see Chapter 2), and the Safari app to surf the Web with your bookmarks (see Chapter 10). With a little help from these apps, you'll soon have your schedule whipped into such shape that it will be humming along like a finely tuned German automobile.

Keep in mind that you can use iTunes to synchronize your iPod touch apps with the calendars, contacts, notes, e-mail accounts, and bookmarks you've already organized on your computer. If you're a Mac user, you have it easy: You can use the free iCal and Address Book applications to manage your calendars and contacts, the free Mail application to manage e-mail, the free Notes Dashboard Widget for notes, and the free Safari Web browser to manage your bookmarks. All these applications are provided with Mac OS X. You can also sync contacts from Microsoft Entourage, Yahoo! Address Book, and Google Address Book, as well as sync calendars from Entourage.

If you're a Windows user, you can sync your contacts and e-mail accounts with Microsoft Outlook 2003 or 2007, Yahoo! Address Book and Yahoo! Mail, Google Address Book and Gmail, Windows Address Book (Outlook Express), AOL (e-mail only), or Vista Contacts. You can sync calendars and notes with Outlook and use Microsoft Internet Explorer or Apple Safari to manage bookmarks. The iPod touch can also use the Exchange ActiveSync protocol to sync e-mail, calendars, and contacts with Microsoft Exchange Server 2003 Service Pack 2 or Exchange Server 2007 Service Pack 1. For many e-mail accounts, the settings automatically appear, like magic.

If you signed up for Apple's MobileMe service (formerly the .Mac service, now www.me.com), you can automatically keep your iPod touch synchronized along with several computers and iPhones, all at once, with the latest e-mail, bookmarks, calendar entries, and contacts, as I describe in the "Going MobileMe to Sync Your iPod touch" section in this chapter.

What's cool about cloud computing Web services like MobileMe, Microsoft Exchange, and Yahoo! Mail is that their e-mail services *push* e-mail messages to your computer and your iPod touch so that they arrive immediately, automatically. Other types of e-mail account services let you *fetch* e-mail from the server — you must first select the account in Mail on your iPod touch before your iPod touch can actually retrieve the e-mail.

You probably already know how to manage your calendar activities and your contacts on your computer. In fact, you're probably knee-deep in contacts, and your calendars look like they were drawn up in the West Wing. If not, visit the Tony's Tips section of my Web site (www.tonybove.com) for advice on using MobileMe and on adding and editing contacts and calendar information on your Mac (with Address Book and iCal) or Windows computer (with Outlook). I also explain how to use third-party utilities to manage personal information on your iPod touch.

Syncing Your Personal Info Using iTunes

You can sync your personal information between your computer and your iPod touch in two ways: either through iTunes, or wirelessly using MobileMe (if you purchase the MobileMe service) or Microsoft Exchange. Please note that you're not wedded to one method or the other — you can switch between the two any time you want.

MobileMe and Exchange get their write-ups in the next section, while this section tackles the iTunes method. To synchronize your iPod touch with contacts, calendars, e-mail accounts, notes, and bookmarks by using iTunes, follow these steps:

1. **Connect the iPod touch and select its name when it appears in the Devices section of the Source pane.**

   iTunes displays the iPod touch sync options to the right of the Source pane, with the Summary page (under the Summary tab) open.

2. **Click the Info tab.**

   The Info sync options page appears as shown in Figure 6-1, offering the Contacts, Calendars, Web Browser, Notes, Mail Accounts, and Advanced sections. (Not all sections are visible in Figure 6-1.)

Figure 6-1: Synchronize selected contact groups and all calendars with the iPod touch.

3. **Select the option to synchronize contacts.**

   On a Mac: Select the Sync Address Book Contacts check box. You can also sync with Yahoo! Address Book or Google Contacts — click the Configure button to enter your login information. An option to sync with Microsoft Entourage appears if you have the application on your Mac.

   On a Windows PC: Select the Sync Contents With option and choose Yahoo! Address Book, Windows Address Book, Google Contacts, or Outlook from the pop-up menu (refer to Figure 6-1).

4. **Select the All Contacts option or select the Selected Groups option and choose which groups to synchronize.**

   You can synchronize all contacts or just selected groups of contacts. To choose groups, select the check box next to each group in the list; scroll the list to see more groups.

   If you select groups, you can also select the Put New Contacts Created on this iPod Into the Group option, and choose a group for the new contacts you create on your iPod touch.

5. **Scroll the page and select the option to synchronize calendars.**

   On a Mac, select the Sync iCal Calendars check box; an option to sync with Entourage also appears if you have it on your Mac. On a Windows PC, select the Sync Calendars With option and choose Outlook from the pop-up menu.

6. **Select the All Calendars option. (Alternatively, if you're using iCal with Mac OS X, select the Selected Calendars option and choose the calendars to synchronize.)**

   In Windows, you can synchronize all calendars with Outlook, but not selected calendars. With iCal on Mac OS X, you can synchronize all calendars or just those you select. To choose specific calendars, select the check box next to each calendar in the list.

   You can also set the Do Not Sync Events Older Than *xx* Days option, in which you can set the *xx* number of days.

7. **Select the calendar to use for new events entered into your iPod touch (Mac OS X only).**

   If you're using Mac OS X and iCal, you should set the calendar to use for new events you create on your iPod touch. Choose a calendar name in the Put New Events Into the Calendar option. When you create a new event on your iPod touch (as I describe in Chapter 13) and sync it back to your computer, the new event appears in this calendar. This affects only new events — events you modify on your iPod touch retain their calendar information from before.

Because you can't select individual calendars with Outlook in Windows, this option is grayed out — all events you create on iPod touch synchronize with the Outlook main calendar.

8. To synchronize Web bookmarks, scroll down to the Web Browser section and select the Sync Bookmarks option.

On a Mac running OS X, the option is Sync Safari Bookmarks; on a Windows PC, iTunes selects Internet Explorer or Safari for this option, depending on which one is your default browser.

9. To synchronize notes, scroll down to the Notes section.

You can sync the notes you create in the Notes app (see Chapter 2) with the Notes Dashboard Widget on a Mac, or with Outlook on a Windows PC. On a Mac, select the Sync Notes option; on a Windows PC, choose Outlook from the pop-up menu for the Sync Notes With option.

10. To synchronize e-mail accounts, scroll down to see the Mail Accounts section and select the Sync Selected Mail Accounts option.

Mail Accounts, as shown in Figure 6-2, appears below the Calendars section in the Info sync options page. On a Mac, select the Sync Selected Mail Accounts option. On a Windows PC, choose Outlook or Outlook Express from the pop-up menu for the Sync Selected Mail Accounts From option. After selecting the sync option, a list of e-mail accounts appears in the box below the option.

11. Choose the e-mail accounts you want to sync.

To choose accounts, select the check box next to each account in the list; scroll the list to see more e-mail accounts.

12. Click the Apply button to apply the changes. (Alternatively, click Cancel to cancel the changes.)

iTunes starts to synchronize your iPod touch.

13. Wait for the sync to finish and then click the Eject button next to the iPod touch name in the Source pane to eject the iPod touch.

Wait until the iTunes Status pane (at the top) displays the message Sync is Complete.

After setting the synchronization options, every time you connect your iPod touch, iTunes automatically synchronizes it with your personal sync options. Synchronizing an e-mail account to your iPod touch copies *only* the e-mail account setup information; the messages are retrieved by the iPod touch over the Internet. Whether the messages in your inbox appear on your iPod touch *and* on your computer depends on the type of e-mail account you have and how you've configured it.

Figure 6-2: Synchronize e-mail accounts.

If you select a calendar or a group of contacts to be synchronized and later want to remove that particular calendar or group of contacts, deselect the calendar (see the preceding Step 6) or the group (see the preceding Step 4) and then click Apply to resynchronize. iTunes synchronizes only the group of contacts and calendars selected, removing from the iPod touch any that aren't selected.

iTunes also offers Advanced options at the bottom of the Info page (refer to Figure 6-2) for synchronizing your iPod touch from scratch to replace all contacts, calendars, notes, or mail accounts. You can choose which ones you want to replace by selecting the check box next to each option. iTunes replaces the information once, during the next sync operation. After that operation, these Advanced options are automatically turned off.

Going MobileMe to Sync Your iPod touch

MobileMe synchronizes MobileMe e-mail accounts along with contacts, calendars, and bookmarks, on a Web server — also known as *the cloud*. You can then keep your iPod touch synchronized to the cloud wirelessly, without having to connect it to your computer.

The place to start organizing your information is usually your computer. However, if you've already entered contacts and calendars on your iPod touch, sync your contacts and calendars on your iPod touch with iTunes first, as I describe earlier in "Syncing Your Personal Info Using iTunes." Then sync your computer with MobileMe, and then your iPod touch with MobileMe.

Make sure the information you synchronize the very first time to MobileMe is the correct, complete information. You should synchronize your primary source — typically your computer — with MobileMe before synchronizing your iPod touch.

MobileMe first makes its appearance when you set up your iPod touch: An advertisement appears with buttons to try MobileMe. If you skipped the ad (like many people do), you can go to the Apple MobileMe setup page (www.apple.com/mobileme) and sign up for a free trial. After setting up your MobileMe account on a Mac or Windows PC, as described in the next sections, you turn on your MobileMe account on your iPod touch, as I describe in "Setting Up Mail Accounts on Your iPod touch".

Setting up on a Mac

Setting up MobileMe is easy on a Mac: When you sign in to MobileMe for the first time, MobileMe automatically configures Mac OS X Mail on your Mac to send and receive e-mail from your MobileMe account and to synchronize contacts from Address Book and calendars from iCal. If you already set up your iPod touch with a Mac and MobileMe service, automatic synchronization should already be set up on that Mac.

If not, you can set up a Mac to sync with MobileMe at any time. Follow these steps:

1. **Choose System Preferences from the Apple menu, choose MobileMe, click the Account tab, and sign in.**

   If you see the .Mac logo instead (for older versions of Mac OS X), select .Mac and sign in. Follow the onscreen instructions, if they appear.

2. **Click the Sync tab.**

   The Sync options for MobileMe appear, as shown in Figure 6-3.

3. **Select the Synchronize with MobileMe check box and then choose a sync interval from the pop-up menu. (Refer to Figure 6-3.)**

   For the most frequent updates, choose Automatically to sync with MobileMe every 15 minutes.

Figure 6-3: Sync options for MobileMe on a Mac.

4. **Click the check boxes to select information to sync with MobileMe.**

   You can choose to sync just contacts, calendars, bookmarks, or mail accounts, or all of them.

5. **Click the Sync Now button.**

   The sync commences. To make sure your data has synced, go to www. me.com, log in, and click the Contacts and Calendar icons along the top row of icons on the left.

Setting up on Windows

Download and install on your PC the latest version of MobileMe Control Panel for Windows, available from http://support.apple.com/down-loads. MobileMe Control Panel is required to set up and manage MobileMe syncing and manage iDisk settings on a Windows PC.

To set up a Windows PC to sync with MobileMe or to check your sync settings or sync immediately, follow these steps:

1. **From the Windows Start menu, open Control Panel and choose MobileMe Control Panel.**

   The MobileMe panel appears with tabs along the top.

2. **Click the Account tab for the Account pane (if it isn't already visible) and log in with your MobileMe member name and password if you aren't already logged in.**

3. **Click the Sync tab.**

   The sync options appear, as shown in Figure 6-4.

4. **Select the Sync with MobileMe check box and then select a sync interval.**

   For the most frequent updates, choose Automatically to sync with MobileMe every 15 minutes.

5. **Select the check boxes to sync your contacts, calendars, and bookmarks, and then use the drop-down lists to choose which Windows applications you want to use when syncing with these items.**

6. **Click the Sync Now button.**

   The sync starts up. To make sure your data has synced, go to www.me.com, log in, and click the Contacts and Calendar icons along the top row of icons on the left.

Figure 6-4: Sync options for MobileMe on a Windows PC.

When you sync upon a cloud

If your contacts or calendar entries show up in duplicate or triplicate on your iPod touch or computer, as if they were stuck inside of MobileMe with the memory blues again, you probably need to overwrite the data in the MobileMe cloud.

Selecting items to synchronize may not overwrite all the data in the cloud. To overwrite the data stored in the cloud with the data on your computer, open MobileMe (in System Preferences on a Mac, or Control Panel in Windows), click the Sync tab, and then click the Advanced button. (Refer to Figure 6-3 for a Mac, or Figure 6-4 for Windows.) Select the computer you are syncing from in the list at the top and then click Reset Sync Data.

In the dialog that appears, choose an option from the Replace pop-up menu:

- ✔ **On a Mac,** you can choose All Sync Info, Bookmarks, Calendars, or Contacts. (The other choices in the pop-up menu — Key Chains, Mail Accounts, and so on — don't copy over to the iPod touch, but are useful for keeping other computers synchronized.)
- ✔ **In Windows,** you can choose All Sync Info, Bookmarks, Calendars, or Contacts.

After choosing an option from the Replace pop-up menu, click the arrow underneath the Cloud icon to change the animation so that the data arrow points from the computer to the cloud. Finally, click Replace.

This action replaces the data in the MobileMe cloud with the data on your computer. You can also use these steps to go in reverse — replace the data on your computer with the data in MobileMe. To do this, click the arrow so that the animation points the arrow from the cloud to the computer.

Changes you make to contacts, calendars, and bookmarks in your iPod touch are synchronized to the Web server at www.me.com. You can also go to www. me.com and access your information directly with your Web browser.

Setting Up Mail Accounts on Your iPod touch

To set up a Mail account on your iPod touch — including a MobileMe e-mail account (with contacts, calendars, and bookmarks) or a Microsoft Exchange account — follow these steps:

1. **Choose Settings⇨Mail, Contacts, Calendars from the Home screen.**

   The Mail, Contacts, Calendars settings screen appears, with the Accounts section at the top, as shown in Figure 6-5 (left side).

2. **Tap the Add Account button and then tap the account type from the list of account types that appears.**

   Your choices are Microsoft Exchange, MobileMe, Gmail, Yahoo! Mail, AOL, or Other, as shown in Figure 6-5 (right side). After tapping the account type, the New Account screen appears for Exchange, MobileMe, Gmail, Yahoo! Mail, and AOL accounts, and the Other screen appears for Other accounts.

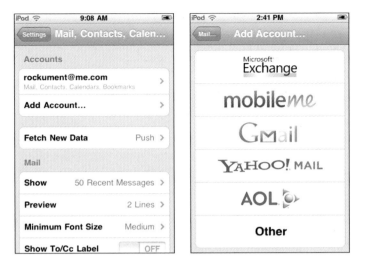

Figure 6-5: Tap Add Account (left) to see the list of account types (right).

3. **Enter your account information as follows:**

MobileMe, Gmail, Yahoo! Mail, or AOL: Enter your name, username, password, and optional description in the New Account screen, and then tap Save in the upper-right corner. If the account is verified, you're done for a Gmail, Yahoo! Mail, or AOL account and you can skip the rest of these steps — the Mail, Contacts, Calendars settings screen appears with the new account listed in the Accounts section. For MobileMe, your iPod touch displays account's settings screen. (If your account doesn't verify, try Steps 2 and 3 again.)

Exchange: Enter your name, username, domain (optional), password, and optional description in the New Account screen, and then tap Next in the upper-right corner to move on to the Exchange account's settings screen. Microsoft's Autodiscovery service kicks in to check your user name and password to determine the address of the Exchange server. If it can't find the server's address, a dialog appears for you to enter it — enter the complete address in the Server field and tap Save.

Other: Tap Add Mail Account on the Other screen for an IMAP (Internet Message Access Protocol) or POP (Post Office Protocol) account. The New Account screen appears; enter your name, username, password, and an optional description, and then tap Save in the upper-right corner to save account information. The iPod touch searches for the account on the Internet and displays the New Account settings screen.

4. **Set your mail account settings in the New Account settings screen as follows:**

   MobileMe or Exchange: Turn on any or all of the items you want to sync: Mail, Contacts, Calendars, and Bookmarks (MobileMe only). If you sync contacts, calendars, or bookmarks using your MobileMe or Exchange account, syncing them in iTunes is turned off. Any contacts, calendars, and bookmarks on your iPod touch are replaced by the MobileMe or Exchange account versions. You can always return to the account setting's screen to turn them off in order to enable syncing with iTunes. For Exchange, you can set how many days of e-mail you want to sync. Tap Save in the upper-right corner to finish and save your settings.

   Other: Tap IMAP or POP on the New Account settings screen, depending on the type of e-mail account you have — ask your e-mail service provider if you don't know. Then enter or edit the existing account information (also get this information from your service provider if you don't know). Tap Save in the upper-right corner to finish and save your settings. The Mail, Contacts, Calendars settings screen appears with the new account listed in the Accounts section.

5. **When the Sync or Cancel warning appears for MobileMe or Exchange accounts, tap Sync (or Cancel).**

   When you tap the Sync button, MobileMe or Exchange overwrites any existing contacts, calendars, and bookmarks on your iPod touch (or the subset of these that you chose in Step 4). After syncing, the Mail, Contacts, Calendars settings screen appears with the new account listed in the Accounts section.

6. **Tap Fetch New Data on the Mail, Contacts, Calendars settings screen, and tap Off for Push to turn it on (if it isn't already on).**

That's it! Your iPod touch syncs automatically from this point on, with data pushed or fetched from the e-mail account depending on your Push and Fetch settings (see Chapter 11 for details).

Changing and Deleting Mail Accounts

You can temporarily turn off a Mail account on your iPod touch, as well as change its settings or delete it. To turn off a Mail account in your iPod touch temporarily or change account settings, choose Settings⇨Mail, Contacts, Calendars from the Home screen, and then touch the account in the Accounts section to see that account's settings screen. You can then change your account's settings, including the items that are synced with a MobileMe or Exchange account.

To delete the account, scroll down and tap Delete Account. Deleting a Mail account from iPod touch doesn't delete the e-mail account itself or its settings on your computer.

Changes you make to accounts are *not* transferred back to your computer when you synchronize, so it's safe to make changes without affecting e-mail account settings on your computer.

It's way beyond the scope of this book to explain all of the e-mail account and advanced options. Grab your network administrator or Internet service provider and offer free coffee in exchange for help. If you don't have anyone to turn to, visit the tips section of my Web site (www.tonybove.com) for tips on using MobileMe and other e-mail accounts, and changing e-mail account settings on your iPod touch.

Part III
Playing It Back with Interest

The 5th Wave   By Rich Tennant

"It's like any other pacemaker, but it comes with an internal iPod docking accessory."

*H*ere's the big playback for your efforts. This part shows you how to play music, TV shows, movies, podcasts, audio books, and slide-shows on your iPod touch.

Chapter 7 is all about playing songs. I show you how to find songs, control the playback and volume, shuffle and repeat songs and albums, and create playlists right on your iPod touch.

Next, Chapter 8 shows you to how to locate and play videos, including movies, TV shows, and YouTube videos. You can skip forward or back-ward, scale the picture to fit the display, and bookmark your favorite sections. I also show you how to play podcasts and audio books.

Then, in Chapter 9, you find out all about synchro-nizing photo albums with your iPod touch, zoom-ing into photos, sharing them with friends, and putting on a slideshow.

The Songs Remain the Same

*E*ven though the iPod and iTunes have irrevocably changed the entertainment industry and how you enjoy music, one thing remains the same: You still play songs. You just play them with more *panache* on your iPod touch.

You can pick any song that you want to hear at any time. You can also shuffle through songs to get an idea of how wide your music choices are or to surprise yourself or others. Browse by artist and album, select a playlist, and even create playlists on-the-fly — this chapter explains it all.

Locating "A Song for You"

With so many songs on your iPod touch, finding a particular song by its title may take longer than finding it another way — like finding a needle in a haystack or even trying to find "Needle in a Haystack" by The Velvelettes. It may be faster to locate albums by cover art or to find songs by searching for artist (or composer), genre, album, or playlist. You can browse your music any number of ways without interrupting the music you're playing.

Going with the Cover Flow

Cover Flow (also called the *cover browser*) lets you flip through your cover art to select music alphabetically by artist. Choose Music from the Home screen and then turn the iPod touch quickly to view it horizontally. This movement changes the display to landscape mode and displays the cover browser, as shown in Figure 7-1.

Slide your finger across the album covers to scroll swiftly through the music library, or tap to the right or left of the cover art in the foreground to move forward or backward an album cover at a time.

Tap the Play button in the lower-left corner (shown in Figure 7-1) to start playing the first song in the foreground album; the Play button turns to a Pause button so that you can tap it again to stop playback. Tap the *i* button in the lower-right corner (or tap the foreground cover art) to list the songs in that album. Then you can tap a song to start playing it.

Figure 7-1: Cover Flow: the cover browser.

Touching artists and albums

You can quickly and easily locate a song by looking up either the song's artist or its album. To browse music by artist, tap the Music icon on the Home screen and tap the Artists icon along the bottom row of the Music screen. A scrollable list of artists appears, with an alphabet listed vertically along the right side, as shown in Figure 7-2.

Tap any letter in the alphabet shown on the right to scroll the list directly to that letter. Tap an artist name to see a list of albums or songs by that

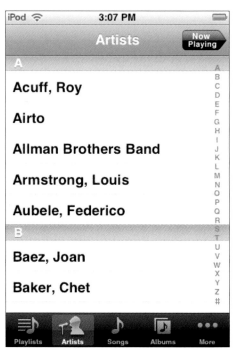

Figure 7-2: Locate an artist's albums and songs.

artist. (You see multiple albums if more than one album is available — tap the album name to select the album.) Tap a song title to start playing the song.

To browse music by album title, tap the Albums icon along the bottom row of the Music screen. Albums appear in a scrollable list with the album cover on the left side and an alphabet listed vertically along the right side, as shown in Figure 7-3.

Slide your finger up and down the alphabet to scroll quickly, or tap any letter in the alphabet to scroll the list directly to that letter. Tap an album title or its cover art to see a list of songs in the album. Tap a song title to start playing the song.

Figure 7-3: Browse by album title.

Choosing a playlist

When you synchronize your iPod touch with your entire iTunes library, your iTunes playlists are included. Well, that makes sense, doesn't it? To browse music by playlist on your iPod touch, tap the Music icon on the Home screen and tap the Playlists icon along the bottom row of the Music screen. A scrollable list of playlists appears. Tap a playlist title to see a list of songs in the playlist and tap a song title to start playing the song.

The songs in the playlist are in the order defined for the playlist in iTunes. But don't despair for lack of something new — you can create playlists in your iPod touch, as I describe later in this chapter.

Tapping song titles and more

To locate songs by title, tap the Music icon on the Home screen and tap the Songs icon along the bottom row of the Music screen. A scrollable list of songs appears with an alphabet listed vertically along the right side. Slide your finger up and down the alphabet to scroll quickly, or tap any letter in the alphabet to scroll the list directly to that letter. Tap a song title to start playing the song.

You can also find music by composer or genre by tapping the More icon along the bottom row of the Music screen. You can then select Composers to see an alphabetical list of composers, or Genres to see all the genres of the songs in your iPod touch. Tap either a composer or a genre to see a list of songs.

Controlling Song Playback

To play a song, tap the song title (or the Play button in Cover Flow).

When the song finishes, the iPod touch plays the next song in the sequence that appeared in the Playlists, Artists, Songs, or Albums screen you chose it from. For example, if you chose a song in the Songs screen, the next song would be the next one in sequence in the Songs screen. If you chose the last song on an album in the Albums screen, the iPod touch stops after playing it. If you chose a song from a playlist on the Playlists screen, the next song would be the next one in the playlist, and after playing the last song it also stops playing, as with an album. (See the "Repeating songs" section later in this chapter to find out how to repeat albums and playlists.)

Whenever you play a song, you see the album cover associated with the song on the Now Playing screen. You also see the buttons for playback control — Previous/Rewind, Play/Pause, and Next/Fast-Forward. (See Figure 7-4.) Slide your finger along the volume slider at the bottom of the display to change the volume.

Tap the Next/Fast-Forward button once to play the next song in sequence, and tap the Previous/Rewind button once at the beginning of a song, or twice during the song, to play the previous song. You can fast-forward through a song by touching and holding down on the Next/Fast-Forward button, and you can rewind a song by touching and holding down on the Previous/Rewind button.

You can tap the bullet-list button in the upper-right corner if you want to display a list of the album's contents. You can then tap the title of another song on the album to start playing that song.

Figure 7-4: The Now Playing screen.

To return to menus and make other selections when playing a song, tap the left-arrow button in the upper-left corner of the display.

Tap underneath the left-arrow button or the album title while a song is playing to show more buttons and the scrubber bar for navigating through the song, as shown in Figure 7-5 — and if lyrics are available in the iTunes information, lyrics also appear.

To skip to any point in a song, drag the playhead along the scrubber bar. To start a song over from the beginning, drag the playhead on the scrubber bar all the way to the left, or tap the Previous/Rewind button once.

If you're viewing another content menu on the iPod touch, tap Now Playing at the top-right corner of the display to go directly to the Now Playing display.

Figure 7-5: Tap under the album title to show more buttons, the scrubber bar, and lyrics.

Repeating songs

If you want to drive yourself crazy repeating the same song over and over, your iPod touch is happy to oblige. (You might want to try repeating "They're Coming to Take Me Away, Ha-Haaa" by Napoleon XIV, a favorite from the old *The Dr. Demento Show* radio broadcasts — and perhaps they will come to take you away.) More than likely, you'll want to repeat a playlist or album, which you can easily do.

Tap underneath the left-arrow button or the album title while a song is playing. The Repeat and Shuffle buttons appear, along with the scrubber bar and lyrics, directly below the top row of buttons. (Refer to Figure 7-5.)

Ordinarily when a song finishes, the iPod touch plays the next song in the sequence that appeared in the Playlists, Artists, Songs, or Albums screen you chose it from. When it reaches the end of that list, it stops — if you chose the last song on an album in the Albums screen, the iPod touch stops after playing it. But if you tap the Repeat button once while the songs are playing, the entire sequence repeats. If you chose an album, the album repeats; if you chose a playlist, the playlist repeats.

After you tap Repeat once to repeat the sequence of songs, the Repeat button shows blue highlighting. Tap the Repeat button again to repeat only the current song — the button changes to include a blue-highlighted numeral 1. Tap it once more to return to normal playback.

Shuffling song order

Maybe you want your song selections to be surprising and unpredictable, and you want your iPod touch to read your mind. You can *shuffle* song playback to play in random order, just like an automated radio station without a disk jockey or program guide.

You can just shake your iPod touch, and it shuffles the songs in the album you are playing. By default, your iPod touch is set to shuffle when shaken (not stirred). Choose Settings➪Music from the Home screen, and touch On for the Shake to Shuffle option to turn it off.

You can also set your iPod touch to shuffle songs across your library. The shuffle algorithm is as random as it gets (not taking into account a fundamental tenet of chaos theory that says a pattern will emerge). When an iPod touch creates a shuffle, it reorders the songs (like shuffling a deck of cards) and then plays them in the new order.

To turn your iPod touch into a random song player, choose Music from the Home screen and tap the Songs icon at the bottom of the display. The song list appears, with Shuffle at the top of the list. Tap Shuffle to turn on Shuffle.

You can also shuffle songs within an album or playlist, which gives you some control over random playback. For example, you can create a playlist for all jazz songs and then shuffle the songs within that jazz playlist. To shuffle songs in an album or playlist, start playing a song in the album or playlist and then tap underneath the left-arrow button or the album title while a song is playing. The Repeat and Shuffle buttons appear, along with the scrubber bar, directly below the top row of buttons (refer to Figure 7-5). Tap the Shuffle button to shuffle songs within the currently playing album or playlist.

You can also set an iPod touch to shuffle any album or playlist *before* playing it. First, select the playlist or album; then tap Shuffle at the top of the list of songs for that playlist or album.

Want to repeat an entire album or playlist but still shuffle the playing order each time you hear it? Start playing a song in the album or playlist and then set your iPod touch to repeat all the songs in the album or playlist as described in the preceding section, "Repeating songs." Then set the iPod touch to shuffle the songs as described in this section.

Creating Playlists on Your iPod touch

If you don't like the playlists copied over from your iTunes library, go out and make some of your own!

You can create a temporary, *On-The-Go* playlist, queuing the songs in the order you want, right on your iPod touch. The selections appear automatically in a playlist appropriately called *On-The-Go,* in the Playlists menu. This option is particularly useful for picking songs to play right before driving a car. (Hel-*lo!* You shouldn't be messing with your iPod touch while driving.)

Your iPod touch can also be a genius about picking songs. If you don't want to go through the process of selecting songs, just select one song and click the Genius button. Your iPod touch takes a look at whatever song you select, and it creates a playlist of songs already on the iPod touch that go along with it.

Ordering playlists On-The-Go

Follow these steps to select songs for your On-The-Go playlist:

1. **Choose Music from the Home screen.**

   The Music screen appears with the Playlists and other icons along the bottom of the display.

2. **Tap the Playlists icon and choose On-The-Go from the Playlists list.**

   The Songs list appears with a plus (+) sign next to each song, as well as an Add All Songs option at the top, as shown in Figure 7-6. If you have only several dozen albums, this list isn't too long, and you can skip to Step 4. If you have a lot more music, narrow your search with Step 3.

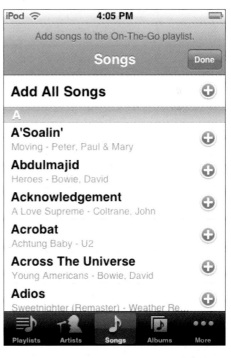

Figure 7-6: Add songs to the On-The-Go playlist.

3. **(Optional) Tap Playlists, Artists, Songs, or More to narrow your search for songs to add to the On-The-Go playlist.**

   Tap an icon along the bottom row (see Figure 7-6) to browse your iPod touch library — tap Playlists to select songs from playlists or entire playlists; tap Artists to browse artists to select songs; or tap More to select songs from albums or compilations, to browse by genre, or to select audio books or podcast episodes.

4. **Tap the plus (+) sign next to a song you want to add to the On-The-Go playlist, or tap the plus sign next to Add All Albums to add all the albums of an artist found in Step 3.**

   As you tap the plus sign for a song, that song is included in the On-The-Go playlist, and it turns gray in the list so that you know it has already been selected. You can tap Add All Albums as an alternative if you want to add all the songs for a particular artist — first browse for that artist in Step 3.

5. **Repeat Steps 3 and 4, adding songs in the order you want them played.**

   You can continue to add songs to the list. Your iPod touch keeps track of the On-The-Go playlist until you clear it (as I describe a bit later in this section) or synchronize your iPod touch, as I describe in Chapter 5.

6. **Tap the Done button when you're finished adding songs.**

   The Done button appears in the upper-right corner while you select songs, just waiting for you to finish. After touching Done, you return to the list of songs in the On-The-Go playlist, as shown in Figure 7-7.

7. **To start playing the On-The-Go playlist, tap any song.**

   Scroll up or down the list (see Figure 7-7) to choose a song, and tap the song title to play the playlist starting from that song. You can tap Shuffle to shuffle the songs in the playlist.

The songs in the playlist are in *playlist order* (the order you added them). You can change that order by tapping the Edit button (see Figure 7-7), which displays the Edit screen with a Move icon (three horizontal bars, like half of an I-Ching symbol) on the far right side of each song. Drag the Move icon for a song to move it up or down the list. Then tap the Done button at the top of the Edit screen.

You can also add entire playlists, entire albums, or everything by an artist to the On-The-Go playlist. In Step 4, tap the Playlists, Artists, or More icon followed by the Albums selection to show one of those menus, and then select a playlist, album, or artist. Finally, tap All Songs at the top of the list of song selections.

After creating the On-The-Go playlist, it remains defined in your iPod touch until you clear it. It turns out that when you synchronize your iPod touch with your iTunes library, doing so copies the On-The-Go playlist to your iTunes library so that you don't lose it. (You can rename it there.) That means you no longer need that particular On-The-Go playlist on your iPod touch, and it's automatically cleared so that you can start creating a new one.

You can also clear the On-The-Go playlist completely in one step: Just tap the Clear button. (See Figure 7-7.) To remove just one or a few songs from the On-The-Go playlist, repeat Steps 1 and 2 earlier in this section and then follow these steps:

1. **Tap the Edit button (see Figure 7-7).**

   The Edit screen appears with circled minus (–) signs appear in front of each song title.

2. **Scroll the list to find the item you want to delete.**

3. **Tap the minus (–) sign next to the song to remove it; then tap the Delete button.**

   The red Delete button appears after you touch the circled minus sign.

4. **Repeat Steps 2 and 3 to find and remove each item from the playlist.**

   When you remove songs, they disappear from the On-The-Go playlist one by one. The songs themselves are not deleted and are still in your iPod touch.

5. **Tap Done at the top of the Edit screen to finish editing the list.**

Figure 7-7: The On-The-Go playlist ready to play (or be cleared).

Consulting the iTunes Genius

The Genius button and its sidekick, the Genius sidebar in iTunes, work with the iTunes Store to match up your tastes to other iTunes users using a technique called *collaborative filtering*. The Genius working behind the scenes in the store analyzes the music and video in other people's iTunes libraries — people who also have the same song or video you selected (if they also turn on the Genius feature in iTunes). The Genius sidebar appears next to the List pane in iTunes, and it informs the online store about the items you select whenever it's open. It then shows you music and video that other listeners purchased when they purchased the items you're playing. All of this information is shared anonymously.

For the Genius feature to work in your iPod touch, you must first give iTunes permission to scan your music library and catalog your iTunes collection, and then you need to sync your iPod touch (as I describe in Chapter 5). The scanning process may take a few minutes or (for very large collections) a few hours, but you can continue using iTunes while it scans your music. To do this, open the sidebar by clicking the Show/Hide Genius Sidebar button in the lower-right corner of the iTunes window. (Refer to Chapter 4). Then click the Turn on Genius button in the sidebar, enter your Apple ID and password for your iTunes Store account, and click Continue.

If you don't have an iTunes Store account yet, select the Create a New iTunes Store Account option and see Chapter 4 for further instructions on creating an account.

After you have enabled the Genius sidebar, you can turn off the Genius feature in iTunes by choosing Store➪Turn Off Genius, and turn it back on by choosing Store➪Turn On Genius. If you add new music to your iTunes library, you can tell iTunes to immediately update the Genius feature with new information by choosing Store➪Update Genius.

When you have the Genius sidebar open, iTunes transmits information to the store about the selection you're playing. To hide the Genius sidebar (and stop transmitting this information), click the Show/Hide Genius sidebar button in the bottom-right corner of the iTunes window.

In your iPod touch, the Genius feature recognizes the song or video you selected, but you must have enough songs or videos on your iPod touch that match the Genius collaborative filtering technique (such as songs purchased by other people who also played the song you are playing).

To create a Genius playlist on your iPod touch, choose Music from the Home screen and follow these steps:

1. **Locate and start playing a song to base the Genius playlist on.**

   The Now Playing screen appears when the song is playing.

2. **Tap the Now Playing screen to see the control buttons.**

   Tap underneath the left-arrow button or the album title while a song is playing. The Repeat, Genius, and Shuffle buttons appear underneath the scrubber bar directly below the top row of buttons. (Refer to Figure 7-5.) The Genius button is the one in the center sporting the atom icon.

3. **Tap the Genius button.**

The Genius playlist appears as shown in Figure 7-8, with New, Refresh, and Save buttons at the top. You can flick your finger to scroll the list. The Genius playlist can be as long as 25 songs. Tap any song to start playing the playlist from that song.

4. **(Optional) Refresh the Genius playlist by tapping Refresh.**

   Refreshing a playlist changes it to include different songs based on the same song you played (depending on how many similar songs you have in your iPod touch).

5. **Save the Genius playlist by tapping Save.**

   The playlist is saved in the Playlists section of your iPod touch using the title of the song it is based on. The playlist is copied back to your iTunes library when you sync your iPod touch. That's all you need to do — the next steps are optional.

   If you subsequently refresh a saved Genius playlist before syncing, the saved playlist is refreshed and you lose the previous version of it.

6. **(Optional) Create a new Genius playlist by tapping New and then selecting a new song to base it on.**

Figure 7-8: The Genius playlist created from the song "Dreaming with a Broken Heart" by John Mayer.

After touching New, the song list appears for selecting a song. Choose a song, and your iPod touch creates a new Genius playlist and starts playing the song, displaying the Now Playing screen.

7. **(Optional) After Step 6, return to the Genius playlist by tapping the left-arrow button in the top-left corner of the Now Playing screen.**

You can refresh any Genius playlist, whether you created it in iTunes and synced to your iPod touch or you created it directly on your iPod touch. Select the playlist and tap Refresh at the top of the list (or tap Delete to delete the list).

TIP

You can set an iPod touch to create a Genius playlist based on a song before you actually start playing the song itself. Just choose Music from the Home screen and then tap Playlists in the bottom-left corner of the display. Tap Genius at the top of the list of playlists, and a list of songs appear. Select a song, and your iPod touch creates a Genius playlist based on it and then starts playing the song you selected. To return to the Genius playlist, tap the left-arrow button in the top-left corner of the Now Playing screen.

In search of the lost chord

If you don't like the music, go out and make some yourself! You can look for the chord the guitar player is playing in a song, and you can try to play it yourself with PocketGuitar (available in the App Store), an app that turns your iPod touch into a virtual guitar. You can press and strum strings with your fingers on the iPod touch screen.

For anyone who plays guitar or wants to play one, you can't beat the value of GuitarToolkit, an iPod touch app (available in the App Store) that provides a chromatic tuner, a chord finder, a metronome, and pitch reference tones. The tuner itself (see figure with the meter) is worth the price ($9.99 as of this writing) and is far more convenient than carrying a separate tuner. The chord finder lets you quickly cycle through chords and see the fingering for each chord. Slide your fingers across the iPod touch screen to strum the chord. The scales feature offers a playable fretboard (see figure with the guitar fretboard) to hear what each note sounds like, and the metronome lets you dial in an exact count in beats per minute (BPM) or tap along to a song to get the tempo.

Adjusting and Limiting the Volume

Because an iPod touch can be quite loud when set to its highest volume, I recommend turning down the volume before using headphones.

To adjust volume, follow these steps:

1. **Play something on the iPod touch.**

2. **While the content is playing, tap the lower portion of the display and slide your finger on the volume slider.**

   After tapping the lower portion of the display while playing something, the volume slider with a silver knob appears on the iPod touch screen at the bottom of the display underneath the playback controls. (Refer to Figure 7-4.) Use your finger to slide the knob to the right to increase the volume or to the left to decrease the volume.

You can also limit the highest volume for your iPod touch to be lower than the actual maximum. This limit can help protect your hearing while you're listening to content from sources with different volume levels. Follow these steps:

1. **Choose Settings⇨Music from the Home screen.**

2. **Choose Volume Limit from the Music settings screen.**

   A volume slider appears with a silver knob.

3. **Slide your finger on the volume slider to limit the volume.**

   Slide the knob with your finger to the right to increase the volume or to the left to decrease the volume.

4. **Tap the Music button in the upper-left corner of the display to set the limit and return to the previous menu, or, if you want, tap the Lock Volume Limit button to lock the volume limit.**

   If you accept the new limit without locking it, you get to skip the next step; you're done. The lock is useful for locking the volume limit so others can't change it (such as your children). However, it also means that you have to enter the volume limit code to unlock the iPod touch in order to change the volume limit.

5. **Set the Volume Limit Code for locking the volume limit.**

   If you tapped the Lock Volume Limit button to lock the volume limit, your iPod touch displays four squares for entering a code number. Tap the calculator-style number pad to type numbers for your code and be sure to make up a code that you can remember! (If you don't want to enter a code, tap the Cancel button in the upper-left corner.)

Tweaking the Sound

Maybe you want more bone-rattling bass or treble highs that are as clear as a bell. The equalizer allows you to fine-tune sound spectrum frequencies in a more precise way than with the typical bass and treble controls you find on home stereos and powered speakers.

Or maybe some of your songs are just too loud. I don't mean too loud stylistically, as in thrash metal with screeching guitars; I mean too loud for your ears when you're wearing headphones or so loud that the music sounds distorted in your speakers. And some songs are just too soft; you have to increase the volume to hear them and then lower the volume to listen to louder songs. To remedy instances like these, you can set the volume in advance in iTunes.

With songs, audio books, podcast episodes, and videos that you already know are too loud (or too soft), consider setting the volume for those items in advance so that they always play with the desired volume adjustment. You can even set the volume for entire albums or podcasts.

To adjust the overall volume of a particular item in advance so that it always plays at that setting, perform the following steps in iTunes:

1. **Select one or more items in your iTunes library.**

   To set the volume in iTunes for multiple songs, you can select an entire album in Browse view or you can select all the songs. To set the volume for a whole podcast, select it instead of individual episodes.

2. **Choose File⇨Get Info.**

   The information dialog appears.

3. **Click the Options tab.**

4. **Drag the Volume Adjustment slider left or right to adjust the volume lower or higher, as shown in Figure 7-9.**

   You can do this while playing the file.

You can standardize the volume level of all the songs in your iTunes library with the Sound Check option in iTunes. This option has the added benefit of applying the same volume adjustment when you play the songs back on your iPod touch.

Peaking with the Sound Check

Sound Check scans the audio files, finds each track's peak volume level, and then uses this peak volume information to level the playing volume of tracks so that they have the same peak volume (this is called *normalization* in audio terms). The sound quality isn't affected, nor is the audio information changed: The volume is simply adjusted at the start of the track to be in line with other tracks. If you mix early '60s music with today's much louder music, like I do, all the songs play at relatively the same volume (so I don't have to adjust the volume) without any loss in quality.

Figure 7-9: Adjust the volume setting in advance for a song.

To enable Sound Check to work in your iPod touch, first follow these steps in iTunes:

1. **Drag the iTunes volume slider to set the overall volume for iTunes.**

   The volume slider is located in the top-left corner of the iTunes window, to the right of the Play button.

2. **Choose iTunes⇨Preferences (Mac) or Edit⇨Preferences (Windows).**

3. **In the iTunes Preferences dialog that appears, click the Playback tab.**

   The Playback preferences appear.

4. **Select the Sound Check box.**

   iTunes sets the volume level for all songs according to the level of the iTunes volume slider.

5. **Click OK.**

   The Sound Check option sets a volume adjustment based on the volume slider on all the songs so that they play at approximately the same volume.

The operation runs in the background while you do other things. If you quit iTunes and then restart it, the operation continues where it left off when you quit. You can switch Sound Check on or off at any time.

To take advantage of volume leveling already set up in your iTunes library, you need to turn on Sound Check in your iPod touch. Choose Settings⇨Music from the Home screen to show the Music settings screen, and tap the Off button next to Sound Check to turn it on. Tap On to turn it back off.

All things being equal (ized)

You can use the iPod touch's built-in equalizer to improve or enhance the sound coming through a particular stereo system and speakers. With the equalizer settings, you can customize playback for different musical genres, listening environments, or speakers.

The iPod touch equalizer uses a bit more battery power when it's on, so you might have less playing time.

The quality of the sound is no better than the speakers you play it on. When you adjust the sound coming from your iPod touch, use your everyday listening environment as a guide. If you tweak the sound specifically for your computer speakers or for your home stereo and speakers, though, remember that with an iPod touch you have other potential listening environments — different headphones, car stereo systems, portable boom boxes, and so on.

To set the equalizer setting, choose Settings⇨Music from the Home screen and tap EQ to display a list of presets. You can scroll the list of presets and tap a preset to select it — a check mark appears next to it after you select it. The equalizer is set to Off until you select one of the presets.

Each equalizer preset offers a different balance of frequencies designed to enhance the sound in certain ways. For example, Bass Booster increases the volume of the low (bass) frequencies; Treble Booster does the same to the high (treble) frequencies.

To see what a preset actually does to the frequencies, choose Window⇨Equalizer in iTunes to open the iTunes equalizer; then select the same preset by name. The faders in the equalizer show you exactly what the preset does.

Find out how to assign standard iTunes presets or your own custom presets to specific songs, audio books, podcast episodes, and videos — and use those presets when playing these items back on your iPod touch — by visiting the tips section of my Web site (www.tonybove.com/tonytips).

8

Bring Videos, Books, and Podcasts

*T*he iPod touch is a terrific video player, with crisp, clear picture quality. Video appears horizontally on the screen (in what's known as *landscape mode*), and if you rotate the iPod touch 180 degrees to the opposite horizontal position, the video adjusts accordingly. All the controls you expect in a DVD player are right on the screen at the touch of a finger.

You can also play audio books and podcasts on this multimedia machine. The iTunes Store offers an amazing selection of TV shows, movies, audio books, and podcasts. (See Chapter 4.) This chapter shows you how to control video playback, skip forward or backward, and scale the picture to fit your screen. It also shows you how to watch videos on YouTube, the free video-sharing Web site started in 2005 that has since exploded with video clips from all corners of the globe.

Everything's Coming Up Videos

Movies, TV shows, and music videos are easy to locate and play. Videos you purchase from the iTunes Store are ready to use, but videos you bring in from other sources may have to be converted first by iTunes to for use on your iPod touch. You can tell if a video needs to be converted by selecting the video in iTunes and checking the Advanced menu: The Create iPod or iPhone version option is grayed out. To convert a video, select the video and choose Advanced➪Create iPod or iPhone Version.

To find out more about why videos need to be converted and how to prepare your own videos and convert imported videos for use with an iPod touch, visit the Tony's Tips section of my Web site (`www.tonybove.com/ tonytips`).

To locate and play a video on your iPod touch, follow these steps:

1. **Tap the Videos icon on the iPod touch Home screen.**

2. **Scroll the Videos screen to see the sections for Movies, TV Shows, Music Videos, and Podcasts (video podcasts only).**

   The video titles are listed in alphabetical order within these sections.

3. **Tap the title of an item to play it.**

Playback under your thumb

Tap the screen to show video controls (as shown in Figure 8-1). You can tap again to hide them.

Tap the Play/Pause button while a video is playing to pause the playback. To raise or lower the volume, drag the volume slider. (See Figure 8-1.)

You can fast-forward through a video by touching and holding down the Next/Fast-Forward button, and you can rewind a video by touching and holding down the Previous/Rewind button.

To skip to any point in a video, drag the playhead along the scrubber bar. To start a video over from the beginning, drag the playhead on the scrubber bar all the way to the left or tap the Previous/ Rewind button (if the video doesn't contain chapters).

Figure 8-1: Tap the screen to use playback controls.

If the video *does* contain chapters, you can skip to the previous or next chapter by tapping the Previous/Rewind or Next/Fast-Forward button. To start playing at a specific chapter, tap the bullet-list button that appears in the top-right corner — but remember, this trick works only if the original video was set up to contain chapters.

To stop watching a video before it finishes playing, tap the Done button in the upper-left corner of the display or press the Home button on the device.

If a video offers an alternative audio language or subtitles, a Subtitles button appears. Tap the Subtitles button and then choose a language from the Audio list, or a language from the Subtitles list, or tap On to turn off subtitles.

Videos are automatically set to remember the playback position when you pause. This feature lets you pause a video or TV episode in iTunes while you synchronize your iPod touch. After syncing, you can continue playing the video or episode on your iPod touch from where you paused. This feature also works the opposite way: If you start playing a video on your iPod touch and then pause, and then you sync it with iTunes, the video retains the playback position so that you can continue playing it in iTunes from where you paused.

You can delete a video directly from your iPod touch by flicking left or right across the video selection in the Videos menu and then tapping the Delete button that appears. Your video is still in iTunes but is deleted from the iPod touch — you can sync the iPod touch again and copy the video back to it (as I explain in Chapter 5). If you delete a rented movie from the iPod touch, it's deleted permanently.

Scaling the picture

Videos are displayed in landscape mode in widescreen format. You can also scale the video picture to fill the screen or to fit within the screen. Tap the Scale button (the one with two arrows facing away from each other — refer to Figure 8-1) or double-tap the video picture itself to switch from one to the other.

Filling the screen may crop the sides, top, and bottom to give you a larger view of the center of the picture. Fitting to the screen assures that the entire picture is shown, but you may see black bars on the sides or top and bottom.

YouTube in Your Hand

The newest and most popular videos in YouTube are right in your hand. All you need to do is connect by Wi-Fi. (See Chapter 4 to set up Wi-Fi.) You can search for and play videos, bookmark favorites for later playback, and share videos with others by e-mail.

Tap YouTube on the Home screen to run the YouTube app. If this is your first visit to the YouTube app, the Featured screen appears, as shown in Figure 8-2. Otherwise, the screen you were viewing when you last used the app appears.

You can tap icons along the bottom of the display to get to other screens, such as Most Viewed, as shown in Figure 8-3, which offers buttons at the top for today's most-viewed videos, the faves for this week, and all of the most-viewed videos.

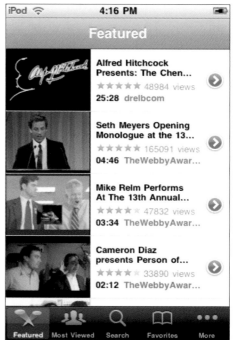

Figure 8-2: Featured videos in YouTube.

After you've saved your favorites as bookmarks (see the "Bookmarking and sharing" section later in this chapter), you can go right to your favorite videos by tapping the Favorites icon. Tap the More icon to see even more screens, including Top Rated (the best of the best), Most Recent (the most recent videos added), and History (all the videos you've played so far). You can also tap the Sign In button to sign into your YouTube account and access the My Videos section of your account.

The History screen offers a Clear button so that you can clear your history at any time.

Running down a stream: Playback control

Tap a selection to play the video. YouTube *streams* the video to your iPod touch — sending it bit by bit — so that you can start playing it immediately.

Tap the video picture to see the controls (see Figure 8-4), which are exactly like the video controls described in the previous section. The progress of the downloaded stream appears in the scrubber bar. Even though you can play the video as it streams, you might want to pause it for a few seconds so that more of the stream is downloaded. You can then play the video without any hiccups.

Bookmarking and sharing

YouTube offers a couple of handy buttons on its videos (see Figure 8-4 for both buttons):

- **Bookmark button (a book icon):** This button appears to the left of the Previous/Rewind button, and you can use it to bookmark the video so that you can easily find it on the Favorites screen.

- **Share button (an envelope icon):** This button is located to the right of the Next/Fast-Forward button. Tap it to bring up the e-mail sending screen to share the video with others via e-mail — see Chapter 11 for details on how to fill out the e-mail message.

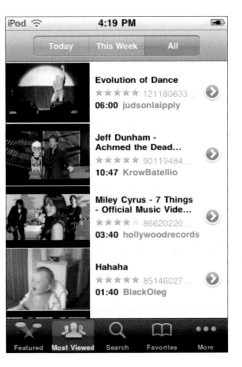

Figure 8-3: Most viewed videos in YouTube for today, this week, and for all time.

Tap the Bookmark button to save a bookmark for the video — the video selection appears in the Favorites screen, which you can access later by tapping the Favorites icon in the bottom row. (The Bookmark button is gray rather than white if the video is already bookmarked.)

You can also bookmark or share the video without playing it, and you can even view information about the video as well as related video selections. Tap the right-arrow button on the right side of each selection (refer to Figure 8-3) to see information about the video and to use the Bookmark or Share buttons.

Figure 8-4: YouTube controls for video playback, bookmarking, and sharing.

To delete entries from your Favorites screen, tap the Favorites icon at the bottom of the display to show your bookmarked favorites, then tap the Edit button in the top-right corner of the screen. The Favorites screen changes to include circled minus (–) signs next to the video selections. To delete a bookmarked video selection, tap the circled minus sign, which then rotates and displays a Delete button over the selection — tap the Delete button. To cancel deletion, tap the rotated circled minus sign again. Tap the Done button in the top-right corner of the Favorites screen to finish editing.

Searching for videos

To search for videos on YouTube, tap the Search icon in the bottom row of icons. Then tap the Search Entry field that appears at the top of the screen. The onscreen keyboard pops up, ready for your search term. (For instructions on using the onscreen keyboard, see Chapter 2.)

If the entry field already has a search term, tap the circled *x* in the right corner of the field to clear its contents. Then tap out the letters of the search term using the onscreen keyboard and tap the Search key on the keyboard. Immediately after tapping Search, video selections from YouTube appear below, as shown in Figure 8-5 (in which I type just **u2** to get the latest U2 music videos).

You can scroll this list by dragging up and down. If a video selection appears that satisfies your search, tap it to play it without further ado.

Figure 8-5: YouTube finds videos based on the search term.

All you have to do is stream

If you're a stream lover (like I am), YouTube isn't nearly enough. You can find streaming Web radio stations and video streams on the Web using apps such as Pandora (radio stations), CBS Sports (live games), and Truveo (TV stations). Your iPod touch needs to be connected to Wi-Fi and the Internet to stream video — see Chapter 4 to get set up.

Pandora lets you type the name of an artist, song, or composer, and Pandora creates a custom station that streams to your iPod touch the music you chose — and more music like it. You can touch the thumbs-up or -down buttons to let Pandora know your musical tastes.

CBS Sports NCAA March Madness on Demand streams live video of every game from the NCAA Division I Men's Basketball Championship.

And with Truveo, it's easy to search for streaming video across sites that include NBC, CNN, The Disney Channel, HBO, Discovery Channel, Comedy Central, PBS, MTV, The Wall Street Journal, YouTube, and Dailymotion, and browse featured videos, top searches, channels, or categories. My favorite feature of Truveo is that it lets me look up the most Twittered videos of the day.

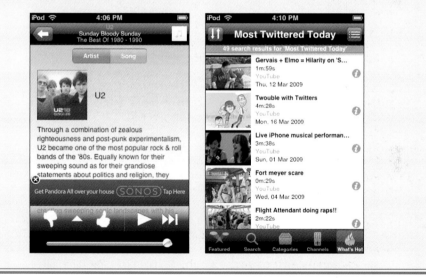

One Chapter at a Time: Audio Books and Podcasts

Audio books are, naturally, organized into chapters or parts. Podcasts are also organized into parts, called *episodes,* and both play the same way. The audio book title or podcast name and episode appear on your iPod touch display along with its cover — similar to a book or album cover.

After syncing your audio books and podcast episodes along with the rest of your content (as I describe in glorious detail in Chapter 5), you can find them in the Music screen: Tap the Music icon on the Home screen and then tap the More icon at the bottom-right corner of the Music screen to see the More screen.

Tap Audiobooks on the More screen and then scroll the Audiobooks screen to select and play an audio book. Tap an audio book on the Audiobooks screen that appears and then tap a chapter or part to play it, starting from that point. The audio book chapters or parts are listed in proper order for each book.

Tap Podcasts on the More screen and then scroll the Podcasts screen to select and play a podcast episode. Podcasts are organized by podcast name (which is like an album name), and episodes are listed within each podcast in the order that they were released (by date). A blue dot appears next to any podcast that has unplayed episodes.

You control the playback of an audio book or podcast episode exactly the same way as a song (see Chapter 7) — you can pause playback by tapping the Play/Pause button, and so on. You can control video podcasts the same way you control videos. (See the section "Everything's Coming Up Videos" in this chapter.)

Audio books and podcasts are automatically set to remember the playback position when you pause. If you pause playback on your iPod touch and then sync with iTunes, you can resume playback at that position on either the iPod touch or in iTunes.

Your Pocket Picture Player

The world is awash in images, from photos and video stills to cartoons and famous paintings. If you like to send and receive images by e-mail, you're going to love the fact that you can now use your iPod touch to share some of the 25,000 images it can hold. This chapter shows you how.

Syncing with Photo Albums and Folders

After importing photos from cameras into your computer, you can organize them into albums or collections. On a Mac, you can use iPhoto (version 4.0.3 or newer) or Aperture. Newer versions of iPhoto let you organize photos by events as well as in albums. On a Windows PC you can use Adobe Photoshop Album (version 2.0 or newer) or Adobe Photoshop Elements (version 3.0 or newer).

You can then set up your iPod touch to sync with your entire photo library or with specific albums in your library so that any changes you make to the library or to those photo albums are copied to the iPod touch. In addition, any images you collect from e-mails on your iPod touch are synced back to the photo library on your computer.

If you don't have these applications, you can use any other photo-editing or photo-organizing software and store your photos in their own folder on your hard drive (such as the Pictures folder in your user's folder on a Mac, or the

My Pictures folder in your My Documents folder in Windows). You can then use iTunes to transfer photos from this folder, treating the folder as a single photo album.

If you want photos in a folder to appear in multiple photo albums on your iPod touch, use the Finder (on a Mac) or Windows Explorer (in Windows) to create subfolders inside the folder and organize your photos and image files inside these subfolders. iTunes copies the subfolder assignments as if they were album assignments. This technique is useful for Adobe Photoshop users who set up Adobe Bridge to organize images.

To find out more about organizing photos into albums, visit the Tony's Tips section of my Web site (www.tonybove.com/tonytips).

Putting images on the iPod touch

To copy images from your computer to your iPod touch using iTunes, follow these steps:

1. **Connect your iPod touch to your computer and then select the iPod touch name in the Devices section of the iTunes Source pane.**

   iTunes displays the Summary page (under the Summary tab of the device's synchronization pages) to the right of the Source pane. (See Chapter 5 for details.)

2. **Click the Photos tab.**

   The Photos sync options appear, as shown in Figure 9-1.

3. **Select the Sync Photos From check box and then pick the source of your photos from the pop-up menu: a photo application, the Pictures (Mac) or My Pictures (PC) folder, or the Choose Folder option.**

   Pick your photo application (such as iPhoto on a Mac, or Adobe Photoshop Album in Windows) from the pop-up menu to synchronize with its library. If you don't use these applications, pick the Pictures folder on a Mac or the My Pictures folder on a PC. If you don't use those folders for your images, pick Choose Folder to use the Mac's Open dialog or the PC's Windows Explorer window to browse your hard drive or other storage media for the folder containing images. After selecting the folder, click Choose (Mac) or OK (Windows).

4. **If you chose a photo application that organizes photos by album, collection, or events, or if you stored images in subfolders in your image folder, select one of the following options below the Sync Photos From check box:**

   • *All Photos and Albums:* Copies all photos and albums (or collections) from the library or folder selected in Step 3.

Figure 9-1: Sync your iPod touch with photo albums.

- *Events:* If you chose a photo application that organizes photos by events (such as iPhoto), you can select All (for all events) or the name of an event from the pop-up menu for the Events option.

- *Selected Albums:* Lets you choose which photo albums from the library (or subfolders from the folder) selected in Step 3 you want to copy. The idea here is to scroll the list box to see all the photo albums or collections in your library (or subfolders in your folder) and then select the check box next to each one you want to copy. (In Figure 9-1, you can see that I decided to copy the subfolders named John and Jimi2 and Rick Wedding from the My Pictures folder.)

5. **Click the Apply button to apply changes and click the Sync button if synchronization hasn't already started automatically.**

   iTunes copies the photo library or albums you selected to your iPod touch (and deletes all other photos from the iPod touch).

No matter what photo application you use, you can save photos as image files in a folder on your hard drive and then bring them into your iPod touch whenever you want. It's rare for an iPod touch to meet an image file format it doesn't like. On a Mac, you can use JPEG (JPG), GIF, TIFF (TIF), Pict, PNG, PSD (Photoshop), PDF, jpg 2000, SGI, and BMP. In Windows, you can use JPEG (JPG), GIF, TIFF (TIF), PNG, and BMP.

Syncing recently saved images

You can save images that you receive via e-mail on your iPod touch — and even save *screen shots* of the iPod touch screen — in a special photo album on your iPod touch called Saved Images. (I describe how to save images and screen shots later in this chapter.)

To synchronize these new images back to your computer, connect your iPod touch to your computer as you normally would to sync it.

On a Mac, iPhoto pops up automatically — click the Import All button, or select the pictures you want and click the Import Selected button. After importing the pictures into the iPhoto library, iPhoto asks whether you want to delete the original pictures from the iPod touch. Click Delete Originals to delete the images from the iPod touch (they're safe in your photo library now) or click Keep Originals to save them on your iPod touch — in case you want to sync them with another computer's photo library. (If you use Aperture rather than iPhoto, you can select the project or folder you want to put the photos in before syncing.)

On a Windows PC, follow the instructions that came with your photo application to import the photos from a digital camera or use the Microsoft Scanner and Camera Wizard, which saves the images to a folder of your choice. (The iPod touch can trick your PC into thinking it's a digital camera.) Most applications also provide an option to delete the photos from the camera (the iPod touch) after importing.

Viewing Images

To view photos and other images on your iPod touch, follow these steps:

1. **Click the Photos icon on the Home screen.**

   The Photo Albums screen appears, as shown in Figure 9-2 (left side), with a list of photo albums — including Saved Photos if you've already saved photos or images from e-mail messages received on your iPod touch.

2. **Tap a photo album's name (or the arrow to the right of the name) or tap Photo Library to see all images.**

   Thumbnail images appear, as shown in Figure 9-2 (right side). The Photo Library choice displays thumbnails of *all* the photos and images in your iPod touch. Selecting an album (as I do in Figure 9-2) displays thumbnails of only the photos and images assigned to that album.

3. **Flick your finger to scroll the thumbnails and tap a thumbnail to select a photo.**

   You might have several screens of thumbnails. Flick your finger to scroll the thumbnails and tap one to select it and view it.

Figure 9-2: Tap a photo album or the entire photo library (left) and then tap a thumbnail image (right).

To view a photo in landscape orientation, rotate the iPod touch sideways. The photo automatically changes to fit the new orientation, and expands to fit the screen if the photo itself is in landscape orientation.

To zoom into the photo to see more detail, double-tap the area you want to zoom into. Double-tap again to zoom out. You can also zoom into an area by unpinching with two fingers, and zoom out by pinching. To pan around a photo, drag the photo with your finger.

To move to the next photo in the library, flick horizontally across the photo with your finger. You can flick across to go backward or forward through the album or the entire library.

Tap the full-screen photo to show or hide the navigation controls, as shown in Figure 9-3. You can see the next or previous photos in the album or library by tapping the Previous or the Next buttons that appear when you tap the photo display.

On with the Slideshow

Slideshows are an especially entertaining way of showing photos because you can include music as well as transitions between photos. You can display your slideshow on the iPod touch or on a television by connecting your iPod touch to the TV using the Universal Dock, Component AV Cable, or Composite AV Cable from Apple (available in the Apple Store).

Setting up a slideshow

To set up a slideshow, follow these steps:

1. **Choose Settings⇨Photos from the Home screen.**

   The Photos Slideshow Settings screen appears, as shown in Figure 9-4.

2. **Tap the Play Each Slide For option to set the duration of each slide.**

   You can select ranges from 2 to 20 seconds.

3. **Tap the Transition option to pick a transition to use between photos in the slideshow.**

   The Wipe Across transition is my favorite, but you can select Cube, Dissolve, Ripple, or Wipe Down. Tap the Photos button to return to the Photos Slideshow Settings screen.

4. **Select other preferences as appropriate for your slideshow:**

   - *Repeat:* Repeats the slideshow.

   - *Shuffle:* Shuffles photos in the slideshow in a random order.

5. **Tap the Settings button to return to the Settings screen or press the Home button on the device to return to the Home screen.**

Options

Previous

Next

Figure 9-3: Photo navigation controls.

To set your iPod touch to display properly on a television, choose Settings⟹ Video. You can then turn Widescreen format on or off (depending on your television) and change your TV signal to PAL (Phase Alternating Line) for European and other countries that use PAL as their video standard. NTSC (National TV Standards Committee) is the U.S. standard and set by default.

Playing a slideshow

To hear music along with the slideshow, first tap the Music icon on the Home screen and select a song (see Chapter 7 for details). Then tap the Home button to return to the Home screen.

To play a slideshow, follow these steps:

1. **Tap the Photos icon on the Home screen.**

2. **Tap an album in the Photos screen or tap Photo Library.**

3. **To start the show, tap the Play/Pause button at the bottom of the thumbnail images. (Refer to Figure 9-2, right side.)**

4. **Use the navigation buttons to move back and forth in your slideshow.**

   Tap any image to see the navigation controls (refer to Figure 9-3) to move to the next or previous image.

5. **Press the Home button on the device to stop the slideshow.**

   The Home button returns you to the Home screen. You can also stop a slideshow by tapping the photo image.

Sharing Images

What good is it to collect pictures without sharing them with other people? You can share images in your iPod touch by sending one or more in an e-mail, uploading as many as you want to social networks, and sharing entire photo albums using MobileMe.

Figure 9-4: The Photo Slideshow Settings screen.

Sending an image by e-mail

To send an image in an e-mail, tap the Photos icon on the Home screen, tap a photo album or Photo Library, and choose the image for viewing (refer to Figure 9-2). Then tap the picture to see the navigation controls (refer to Figure 9-3). Tap the Options button in the lower-left corner of the screen to see the Options menu, as shown in Figure 9-5, and then tap the Email Photo button to e-mail the image.

The New Message screen appears with the photo embedded in the message. You can tap in the message field to enter text. Then fill in the To and Subject fields as described in Chapter 11.

You can also use the Options menu to assign the photo to a contact in your Contacts list (see Chapter 13 for details) or use the image as the iPod touch wallpaper (see Chapter 3) as well as sharing it with others using MobileMe (see "Sharing photo albums" later in this section).

Figure 9-5: Choose the option to e-mail the photo.

Selecting and copying multiple images

To select more than one image to copy and paste into another app or to share by e-mail, tap the Photos icon on the Home screen, tap a photo album or Photo Library (refer to Figure 9-2, left side) and then tap the Selection button in the bottom-left corner of the thumbnail images (refer to Figure 9-2, right side). The Select Photos screen appears, showing the same thumbnails. Tap each thumbnail in the Select Photos screen, as shown in Figure 9-6 (left side), to select each image. As you tap each thumbnail, a check mark appears in the thumbnail to indicate that it is part of the selection.

To e-mail the images, tap the Share button, and then tap Email. The Mail app launches and starts a new e-mail message that includes all of the selected images (see Chapter 11 for details on sending e-mails).

To copy the images to another app or paste them in an existing message, tap the Copy button to copy the images. You can paste the images into any app that accepts pasted images — such as a saved e-mail draft message in Mail. Touch and hold to mark an insertion point in the e-mail message (which brings up the keyboard), so that the Select/Select All/Paste bubble appears, as shown in Figure 9-6 (right side). Tap Paste to paste the images into the message.

Figure 9-6: Select images for copying or sharing (left), and paste the images into a draft e-mail message (right).

Saving an image attached to an e-mail

You can also receive images from others by e-mail. (See Chapter 11 for details on how to check your e-mail.) A down-arrow button appears within a message that contains an attached image, as shown in Figure 9-7 (left side). Tap the down-arrow button to download the image to your iPod touch. After the download completes, tap the image itself in the e-mail message, and the Save Image and Cancel buttons appear, as shown in Figure 9-7 (right side). Tap the Save Image button to save the image in your iPod touch photo library (in the Saved Images album) or tap Cancel to cancel. If the message has more than one image (such as three) you can tap a button to save them all (such as Save 3 Images in Figure 9–7, right side).

Figure 9-7: An e-mail with an image attached (left); saving images in your iPod touch (right).

Sharing photo albums

If you've set up a photo album on MobileMe to share with others, you can include any image in your iPod touch in this published album so that others can immediately see it. Tap the Options button as described earlier in the "Sending an image by e-mail" section and then tap the Send to MobileMe button. The iPod touch contacts MobileMe over Wi-Fi and displays a list of the photo albums you've published on MobileMe to share with others. Select the album to include the image.

You can also share images using services such as Facebook and MySpace — both offer iPod touch apps that let you upload images from your iPod touch. See Chapter 13 for a sociable description.

Capturing a screen shot

You too can capture shots of the iPod touch screen and display them in a book or Web site, just as I have. No matter what application you're running, quickly press and release the Sleep/Wake and Home buttons at the same time. The iPod touch screen flashes (and if your volume is up, you can hear a shutter click). This indicates that the screen was saved in the Saved Images album — choose the album in Photos to see the image. You can take as many screen shots as you like. The next time you sync your iPod touch to your computer, your photo application (such as iPhoto) launches to receive these new images.

Part IV
Touching the Online World

The iPod was always in a class by itself as a media player. But the iPod touch takes the concept of playing media to an entirely new level by providing access to the world of online content. Now you can visit Web sites around the world, download songs, play YouTube videos, check your e-mail, and even monitor your stock portfolio.

Chapter 10 spins the Web and shows you how to surf Web pages with Safari. You discover how to search with Google or Yahoo! and interact with Web services to do everything from checking live news feeds to making travel reservations.

Next, in Chapter 11, you find out how to turn your iPod touch into a lean, clean, e-mail machine. You can check e-mails from multiple e-mail accounts, send messages, and manage your e-mail settings.

Then, in Chapter 12, the weather becomes more predictable, your stocks proudly show their charts, and the Earth itself reveals its secrets in satellite and map views — all on your iPod touch.

Surfin' Safari

T he World Wide Web makes the world go 'round a whole lot faster than ever before. I browse the Web for many different kinds of content and services. It's gotten to the point where I now make travel, restaurant, and entertainment reservations, and I purchase everything on the Web, from music, videos, books, and clothing to electronics equipment, garden supplies, groceries, and furniture. I get to track my shipments and purchases, review the latest news, check up on the blogs of my friends and associates, read novels, view slide shows and movies posted on the Internet, and even scan text messages from cell phones — all thanks to the Internet.

I can do all this on my iPod touch, using the Safari browser with a Wi-Fi connection, so I rarely need a laptop when I travel. I can also search using Google or Yahoo! — both services are built into Safari, and you can always browse any other search site.

The iPod touch connects to the Internet through Wi-Fi networks. It can join AirPort and other Wi-Fi networks at home, at work, or at Wi-Fi hotspots around the world, as I describe in Chapter 4.

Take a Walk on the Web Side with Safari

Safari on the iPod touch not only lets you browse through Web sites but also lets you add bookmarks and icons to your Home screen for convenient access. (You can also synchronize those bookmarks with your computer's Web browser, as I describe in Chapter 6.)

Go URL own way

It's a snap to browse any Web site. Just tap out the site's address on the onscreen keyboard. (For instructions on using the onscreen keyboard, see Chapter 2.)

The Web site address is known as a URL (Uniform Resource Locator) and usually begins with `http://www.` followed by the name of the Web site or other characters (such as `http://www.apple.com` or `http://www.tonybove. com/tonytips`). However, you can leave off the `http://www.` part and just go with the rest of the characters of the URL (`apple.com` or `tonybove.com/ tonytips`).

For the blow-by-blow account, check out the following steps:

1. **Tap the Safari icon on the Home screen.**

   The iPod touch displays the last Web page you visited or a blank page, with the rectangular URL entry field at the top-left corner and an oval search entry field in the top-right corner, as shown in Figure 10-1. (If you don't see these two entry fields side by side, tap the status bar at the top of the screen to jump to the top of the Web page.)

2. **Tap the URL field.**

   The onscreen keyboard appears. Above that is an entry field for typing the URL.

3. **If the entry field already has a URL, tap the circled *x* in the right corner of the field to clear its contents.**

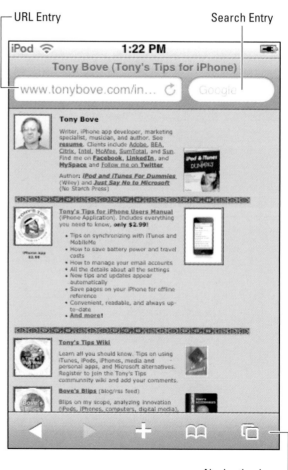

Figure 10-1: The URL and search fields appear at the top of the Web page in Safari.

4. **Tap out the URL for the Web page using the onscreen keyboard.**

   Immediately as you start typing the characters of the URL, you see a list of suggested Web sites in your bookmarks or history list that match the characters you typed so far (as shown in Figure 10-2). You can scroll the suggested list by dragging up and down. If the Web site you want appears, tap it to go directly to the site without further ado. Otherwise, keep typing the URL, including the extension — the keyboard includes a .com button, next to the Go button, for your convenience.

5. **Tap the Go button on the keyboard (or tap Cancel to cancel).**

   When you tap the Go button, your iPod touch closes the keyboard, displays the message Loading in the status bar, and loads the Web page from the Internet, if the page exists. If you mistyped the URL or the page doesn't exist, you get the message Safari can't open the page because it can't find the server. Tap OK and start again from Step 2.

   To cancel entering a URL, tap the Cancel button in the top-right corner of the screen (refer to Figure 10-2).

Figure 10-2: Enter the first characters of the Web site's URL, and suggestions appear below from your history or bookmarks.

To stop a Web page from loading if you change your mind, tap the *x* on the right side of the URL entry field. This *x* turns into a circular arrow after the page is loaded. To reload an already loaded Web page to refresh its contents, tap the circular arrow.

Hanging loose with your bookmarks

If you already have bookmarks saved in your iPod touch, you can go directly to your favorite bookmarked pages. (To add bookmarks to your iPod touch, you can sync bookmarks from your computer's Web browser, as described in Chapter 6, and you can also save bookmarks of pages you visit with your iPod touch, as described in "Bookmarking As You Go," later in this chapter.)

Follow these steps:

1. **Tap the Safari icon on the Home screen.**

   Your iPod touch displays the last Web page you visited or a blank page. A navigation bar sporting various icons and buttons appears along the bottom, as shown in Figure 10-3.

2. **Tap the Bookmarks icon — the one that looks like an open book— in the navigation bar.**

   The Bookmarks screen appears with the special History folder that records your page visits, and other Bookmark-related folders (such as Bookmarks Bar and Bookmarks Menu, provided with the Safari application on Macs and PCs). You can scroll this list by dragging up and down.

3. **Tap a folder to view its contents.**

   For example, tapping Bookmarks Menu opens the folders and bookmarks from the Bookmarks Menu section of Safari on your Mac or PC. Tapping Bookmarks Bar opens the folders and bookmarks in the Bookmarks Bar section. Tapping History opens the history of the Web pages you've visited.

4. **Tap a bookmark to load the Web page.**

   Folders have a folder icon to the left of their names, and actual bookmarks have an open-page icon next to their Web page names. Tap a folder to reveal its contents and tap a bookmark to load a Web page.

Figure 10-3: Use the navigation bar to navigate Web pages and to open and save bookmarks.

You can rotate the iPod touch sideways to view Web pages in landscape (horizontal) orientation, and then double-tap to zoom in or out — Safari automatically fits sections of Web pages (such as columns of text) to fill the screen for easy reading. You can also spread with two fingers to control the amount of zooming.

Pearl diving with Google or Yahoo!

If you've done any Web surfing at all, you already know all there is to know about search engines. They're simply *the* tool for finding Web sites. The two most popular search engines out there — Google and Yahoo! — are built into Safari on your iPod touch.

Google is set up to be your default Web search engine, but you can quickly change that. To choose Yahoo! (or to go back to Google), tap Settings➪ Safari➪Search Engine, and tap Yahoo! or Google. Turning on one search engine turns off the other search engine.

Follow these steps to search with Google or Yahoo! from within Safari:

1. **Tap the Safari icon on the Home screen.**

   The iPod touch displays the last Web page you visited or a blank page. You can find the URL entry field in the top-left corner and the oval search entry field, with Google or Yahoo! in gray, in the top-right corner (refer to Figure 10-1). (If you don't see these two entry fields side by side, tap the status bar at the top of the screen to jump to the top of the Web page.)

2. **Tap the oval search entry field.**

   The onscreen keyboard appears. Above that is the search entry field (with a magnifying glass icon).

3. **Tap inside the search entry field.**

4. **Tap out the letters of the search term using the keyboard.**

   Immediately as you start typing characters, you see a list of suggested bookmarks in your bookmarks folder or history list. You can scroll this list by dragging up and down.

5. **If a bookmark appears that satisfies your search, tap it to go directly to the Web page without further ado. Otherwise, keep typing the search term.**

6. **Tap the Google or Yahoo! button at the bottom-right corner of the keyboard.**

   Doing so closes the keyboard and displays the search results. (*Note:* The Google or Yahoo! button replaces the Go button on the keyboard when searching.)

Let Your Fingers Do the Surfing

After you've found the Web page you want, you can use your fingers to navigate its links and play any media it has to offer. You can also bounce around from previous to next pages in your browsing session, open multiple pages, zoom into pages to see them clearly, and scroll around the page to see all of its sections while zooming.

Scrolling and zooming

To zoom into a Web page in Safari, spread two fingers apart on the screen (unpinch). To zoom back out, bring your fingers together (pinch).

Double-tap the display to zoom into any part of the page. You can also double-tap a column to automatically zoom in so that the column fills the iPod touch display. Double-tap again to zoom back out.

To scroll around the page, touch and drag the page. (If you happen to touch a link, drag the link so that you don't follow the link.) You can drag up, down, or sideways to see the entire Web page; or flick your finger up or down to quickly scroll the page. Use two fingers to scroll within the frame on a Web page or one finger to scroll the entire page.

To jump to the top of a Web page, tap the status bar at the top of the iPod touch screen.

All of these gestures work the same way in either portrait or landscape orientation. To view a Web page in landscape orientation, rotate the iPod touch sideways. Safari automatically reorients and expands the page. To set it back to portrait, rotate the iPod touch again.

It's all touch and go

To follow a link on a Web page, tap the link. Text links are usually underlined (sometimes in blue). Many images are also links you can tap to navigate to another page or use to play media content.

If a link leads to a sound or movie file supported by the iPod touch, Safari plays the sound or movie; if the link points to YouTube, the YouTube app launches to play the video. (See Chapter 7 for sounds and Chapter 8 for videos.)

You can see the link's destination — without following it — by touching and holding down on the link until the destination address appears (next to your finger). You can touch and hold an image to see whether it has a link.

To move to the previous page in your browsing sequence, tap the left-arrow button in the left side of the navigation bar at the bottom of the screen. (Refer to Figure 10-3.) Safari replaces the current page with the previous one. If you've just started browsing and this is the first page you've opened, the left-arrow button is grayed out.

To move to the next page, tap the right-arrow button (to the right of the left-arrow button) in the navigation bar at the bottom of the screen. (Refer to Figure 10-3.) Safari replaces the current page with the next one in the browsing sequence. This button is grayed out unless you've navigated backward to some previous page.

You can always go back to any of the pages you visited by tapping the Bookmarks button in the navigation bar and then tapping History. To clear your History list on your iPod touch, tap Clear.

Surfing multiple pages

Although you can open Web pages one at a time and switch back and forth between them, you can also open several pages and start a new browsing sequence with each page, just like opening separate browser windows or tabs.

Some links automatically open a new page instead of replacing the current one, leaving you with multiple pages open. Safari displays the number of open pages inside the Pages icon in the right corner of the navigation bar at the bottom of the screen. If there's no number on the icon, it means only one page is open.

To open a separate page, tap the Pages icon on the right side of the navigation bar at the bottom of the screen; then tap the New Page button. Safari brushes aside the existing page to display a new one. You can then use your bookmarks, enter a Web page URL, or search for a Web page. (If you change your mind and don't want to open a new page, tap the Done button to cancel.)

To close a separate page, tap the Pages icon on the right side of the navigation bar to display the page thumbnail images and then tap the red circled x in the top-left corner of the Web page thumbnail for the page you want to close. The page disappears.

To switch among open pages, tap the Pages icon to display the page thumbnail images, as shown in Figure 10-4, and flick left or right to scroll the images. When you get to the thumbnail image of the page you want, touch it!

Figure 10-4: Switch among open Web pages.

Interacting with pages

Many Web pages have pop-up menus for making choices. For example, the NextBus Stop Selector site (www.nextmuni.com) offers pop-up menus for selecting the state, the transit agency, and the bus line. To make choices for a pop-up menu, tap the menu. Safari displays a list of possible choices for that pop-up menu (such as a list of bus lines). Choose one by tapping it; you can also flick to scroll the list of choices.

After choosing an option, tap the Done button to finish with that pop-up menu. You can also tap the Previous or Next buttons to move to the previous or next pop-up menu.

Entering text into a Web site — such as reservation information, passwords, credit card numbers, search terms, and so on — is as easy as tapping inside the text field. Safari brings up the keyboard, as shown in Figure 10-5, and you can type the text. You may want to rotate the iPod touch sideways to view Web pages in landscape (horizontal) orientation, so that the keyboard is wider and easier to use.

Figure 10-5: Type the text for a text field on a Web page.

You can move to the next or previous text field by tapping the Next or Previous buttons or by tapping inside another text field. To finish typing with the keyboard, tap the Done button. If you don't like what you typed, use the backspace key to delete it before tapping Done.

After you finish filling out all the required text fields on the page, tap Go on the keyboard (or tap Search, which some pages use rather than Go). If the Web page is a form, tapping Go automatically submits the form. Some Web pages offer a link for submitting the form, which you must tap in order to finish entering information.

Copying text

You may want to copy one or more paragraphs of text from a Web page to paste into another app (such as Notes) or into an e-mail. Although you can e-mail a link to a Web page (as I show you in the "Sending a Web link by e-mail" section in this chapter), you may want to copy a section of text and then paste the section into the message itself.

To copy a section of text from a Web page, touch and hold somewhere within the section (also known as a *long tap*). Safari automatically highlights the section with selection handles on either end, and it displays the Copy bubble (see Figure 10-6). Tap Copy to copy the selection.

Figure 10-6: Copy a selected section of text on a Web page.

If you zoomed into the Web page and the long tap selects only a single word, try zooming out first (pinching) and then trying the long tap (touch and hold) again. You can also make a more precise selection by dragging one of the handles. A rectangular magnifier appears for dragging the handle precisely. After you remove your finger to stop dragging, the Copy bubble appears.

For details on pasting the selected text into apps such as Notes or into an e-mail, see Chapter 2.

Bookmarking As You Go

The best way to keep track of Web pages you've visited and want to visit again is to create bookmarks for the pages. You can then quickly go back to that page by selecting the bookmark. The bookmarks in your iPod touch synchronize with your Safari bookmarks on your Mac, or with your Safari or Internet Explorer bookmarks on your PC, as I describe in Chapter 6.

Saving a bookmark

Follow these steps to save a bookmark:

1. **Browse to the Web page you want.**

2. **Tap the plus (+) sign in the middle of the navigation bar (refer to Figure 10-3).**

The special options menu appears, as shown in Figure 10-7, with the Add Bookmark, Add to Home Screen, Mail Link to this Page, and Cancel buttons.

3. Tap the Add Bookmark button to add a bookmark.

The name of the Web site appears in the title field, ready for editing, along with the onscreen keyboard. Below that is the actual URL for the Web page, and below that, the Bookmarks folder.

4. (Optional) Edit the bookmark's title.

Before saving a bookmark, you can edit its title with the onscreen keyboard. Tap the circled *x* on the right side of the title field to clear its contents, or use the backspace key on the keyboard to erase backward from the end of the title, and type the new title.

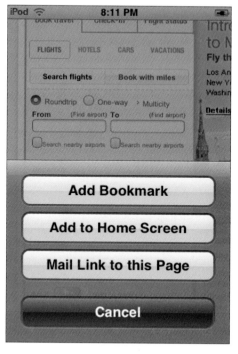

Figure 10-7: Tap the plus (+) sign for the special options menu.

5. (Optional) Choose a bookmark folder.

Before saving a bookmark, you can choose a bookmark folder for saving it; otherwise Safari saves the bookmark in the topmost level of bookmarks. Tap Bookmarks to see the list of bookmark folders — you can flick to scroll the list quickly, or drag it slowly. Select a bookmark folder by touching it.

6. Tap the Save button to save the bookmark or tap Cancel to cancel.

The Save button appears in the upper-right corner of the display, and the Cancel button appears in the upper-left corner.

You can also edit your bookmarks and bookmark folders. Tap the Bookmarks button in the navigation bar and choose the folder to edit or the folder that has the bookmark you want to edit. Then tap the Edit button in the bottom-left corner of the screen. The Edit Bookmarks display appears, with circled minus (–) signs next to the bookmark folders.

You can then do any of the following:

- To make a new folder within the selected folder, tap New Folder. If you want to create a new folder at the topmost level, first tap the Bookmarks button in the upper-left corner to go back to the topmost Bookmarks list, tap the Edit button, and then tap New Folder.

- To delete a bookmark or folder, tap next to the bookmark or folder and then tap Delete.

- To reposition a bookmark or folder, drag next to the item you want to move.

- To edit the name of a bookmark or folder, tap the bookmark or folder and use the onscreen keyboard to type the new title. (Tap the circled *x* in the title field to clear its contents first, if you want.)

- To change where a bookmark or folder is stored, tap the Bookmark Folder field for the selected bookmark or folder and then tap a new folder to hold the folder chosen for editing.

Tap the Done button in the bottom-left corner of the Edit Bookmarks display to finish editing.

Sending a Web link by e-mail

As I describe in Chapter 11, your iPod touch can send e-mail as well as receive it, as long as it's connected to a Wi-Fi network that's connected to the Internet. And if you want to share a Web page you just found with your friend, the steps are simple:

1. **Browse to the Web page and then tap the plus (+) sign in the middle of the navigation bar at the bottom of the screen. (Refer to Figure 10-3.)**

   A special options menu magically pops up from the bottom (refer to Figure 10-7), with the Add Bookmark, Add to Home Screen, and Mail Link to This Page buttons, along with a Cancel button.

2. **Tap the Mail Link to this Page button.**

   Keep in mind that you must have already set up an e-mail account on your iPod touch, as I describe in Chapter 6.

   An e-mail message appears, ready for you to finish composing. The Subject field is already filled in with the Web page name, and the link itself is already inserted in the body of the message. The To and Cc fields are left blank — ready for you to fill in.

3. **Tap the circled plus (+) sign on the right side of the To field to select a name from your Contacts list, or use the onscreen keyboard to enter the e-mail address.**

   See Chapter 11 for details on sending an e-mail.

4. **Tap Send at the top-right corner of the display to send the message.**

Bringing It All Back Home

You can add Web thumbnail icons for your favorite Web pages to the Home screen so that you can access the page with one touch. Web icons appear on the Home screen along with the icons of other apps. (Discover how to rearrange the icons and add multiple screens to the Home screen in Chapter 2.)

Follow these steps to add a Web site to your Home screen:

1. **Browse to the Web page you want.**

2. **Tap the plus (+) sign in the middle of the navigation bar.**

   The special options menu appears, with Add Bookmark, Add to Home Screen, Mail Link to this Page, and Cancel buttons (refer to Figure 10-7).

3. **Tap the Add to Home Screen button.**

   The name of the Web site appears in the title field, ready for editing, along with the keyboard. The icon to be added to the Home screen — a thumbnail image of the site, or a graphic image defined by the site for this purpose (usually a logo) — appears to the left of the title field.

4. **(Optional) Edit the Web icon's title.**

   Before saving a Web icon to the Home screen, you can edit its title with the keyboard. Tap the circled *x* on the right side of the title field to clear its contents, or you can use the backspace key on the keyboard to erase backward from the end of the title and then type the new title.

5. **Tap the Add button to add the Web site icon, or tap Cancel to cancel.**

   The Add button appears in the upper-right corner of the display, and the Cancel button appears in the upper-left corner.

11

The Postman Always Beeps Once

*Y*our e-mail is just a touch away. The Mail app on your iPod touch can display richly formatted messages, and you can send as well as receive photos and graphics, which are displayed in your message along with the text. You can even receive Portable Document Format (PDF) files, Microsoft Word documents, and Microsoft Excel spreadsheets as attachments and view them on your iPod touch.

The Mail app on your iPod touch can work in the background to retrieve your e-mail when you're connected to Wi-Fi. If you signed up for Apple's MobileMe service (formerly the .Mac service, now www.me.com), as I describe in illustrious detail in Chapter 6, your iPod touch receives e-mail the instant it arrives in the mailbox on the MobileMe service. Services such as MobileMe, Microsoft Exchange, and Yahoo! Mail *push* e-mail messages to your iPod touch so that they arrive immediately, automatically. You get a single beep when your mail has arrived (unless you turned off the New Mail sound, as I describe in Chapter 3).

Other types of e-mail account services let you *fetch* e-mail from the server — when you select the account in Mail on your iPod touch, Mail automatically starts fetching the e-mail, and you can browse your e-mail accounts or even use other apps while Mail fetches messages. You can also tell Mail to fetch more messages by tapping the Fetch (circular arrow) icon on the lower-left corner of the Mail, Mailboxes, or message screens.

Checking E-Mail

You know that you have unread e-mail if the Mail icon on the iPod touch Home screen shows a number — this is the number of unread messages in your inboxes. As e-mail is pushed (or fetched) to your iPod touch, this number increases until you read the messages. Tap the Mail icon to start the Mail app.

If you've set up an e-mail account, a list of mailboxes appears for that account, as shown in Figure 11-1 (left side). If you've set up more than one e-mail account, Mail displays the Accounts screen, listing the e-mail accounts you synchronized with your iPod touch (see Figure 11-1, middle). Tap an account in the Accounts screen to view the mailboxes for that account (see Figure 11-1, right side). (See Chapter 6 for details on synchronizing, setting up, deleting, and changing settings for e-mail accounts.)

Figure 11-1: A MobileMe account's mailboxes (left); multiple e-mail accounts (middle), and the mailbox (Inbox) of an AOL e-mail account (right).

Next, tap Inbox in the list of mailboxes. A list of incoming message headers appears, as shown in Figure 11-2, with the sender's name, subject, and the first sentence or two of each message, along with a blue dot if the message hasn't been read yet.

The message is the medium

Tap a message header to read the message. You can scroll the message by flicking or dragging your finger, and zoom into and out of the message by unpinching and pinching with your fingers. You can also zoom directly into a column in the message by double-tapping the message, and zoom out by double-tapping it again.

If the e-mail includes an attachment, a button appears within the message showing the icon of an attached file and a right arrow, as shown in Figure 11-3 (left side) — to view the attachment, just tap the right arrow. If the format of the attached file is one of the supported formats (which include files that have the extensions `.doc`, `.docx`, `.htm`, `.html`, `.pdf`, `.txt`, `.xls`, or `.xlsx`), Mail downloads and opens the attachment as shown in Figure 11-3 (right side); if not, Mail displays a document icon with the name of the file — but you can't open it.

You can see all the recipients of a message (except Bcc, or *blind carbon copy,* recipients) by opening the message and tapping the blue word Details in the top-right corner of the message. Tap a name or e-mail address that appears to see the recipient's contact information. Tap Hide to hide the recipients.

Figure 11-2: Check out your incoming messages. A blue dot indicates an unread message.

You can add the sender or recipient to your Contacts list on your iPod touch by tapping the name or e-mail address. A screen appears with the Email, Create New Contact, and Add to Existing Contact buttons. Tap Create New Contact to create a new contact (or tap Add to Existing Contact if you want to add the information to an existing contact). Tap the Email button to send an e-mail to that recipient's address. (See the "Sending E-Mail" section, later in this chapter.)

Links appear in a message underlined in blue, and images embedded in the message may also have links. Tapping a link can take you to a Web page in Safari, open a map in Maps, or open a new pre-addressed e-mail message in Mail. To return to your e-mail, press the Home button on your device and tap the Mail icon.

You can mark a message as unread so that it stays in your Inbox: Open the message, tap the blue word Details in the top-right corner, and tap the blue Mark as Unread text next to the blue dot inside the message. The message is marked as unread — a blue dot appears next to the message header in the mailbox list until you open it again.

Previous Next

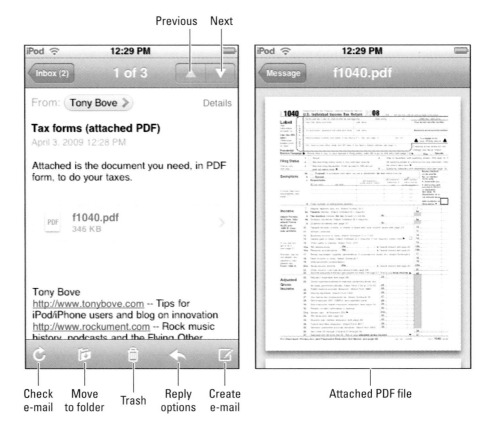

Check   Move   Reply   Create
e-mail   to folder Trash options e-mail   Attached PDF file

Figure 11-3: The e-mail message appears with an attachment (left side); tap the right arrow to view the attachment (a PDF file).

Deleting a message

To delete an open message, tap the Trash icon at the bottom center of the message display. Mail deletes the message from your iPod touch (but *not* from your computer or mail server unless it's set up that way — see Chapter 6) and displays the next message in sequence. You can also move to the previous or next message by tapping the up and down arrows in the top-right corner.

You can also delete a message without opening it. In the list of message headers, drag your finger across a message header and tap the Delete button that appears.

To delete a list of messages quickly, choose the mailbox (such as Inbox) and tap the Edit button in the top-right corner of the screen. The messages appear with empty circles next to them. Tap each message so that a check mark appears in the empty circle. After checking off the messages to delete, tap the Delete button in the bottom-left corner.

Sending E-Mail

You can use the Mail app to reply to any message instantly and send e-mail to any e-mail address in the world. You can even send a message to a group of people without having to select each person's e-mail address.

To send an e-mail, follow these steps:

1. **Tap the Mail icon on the Home screen.**

   The Accounts screen appears if you've set up more than one e-mail account, and you should look at Step 2; otherwise, the mailboxes appear for your account, and you can skip to Step 3.

2. **(Optional) Choose an e-mail account from the Accounts screen for sending the e-mail.**

   You can skip this step if you have only one e-mail account. If you have several e-mail accounts on your iPod touch, you can select one of them, or you can use the default account for sending e-mail. (See the section "Message Settings and Sending Options," later in this chapter, to set the default account.) You can also defer this decision until Step 6.

3. **Tap the pencil-document icon in the lower-right corner of the Mail screen.**

   The New Message screen appears, as shown in Figure 11-4, along with the onscreen keyboard. If you have multiple accounts set up on your iPod touch, the default account for sending e-mail appears in the Cc/Bcc, From field.

4. **Enter the recipient's e-mail address in the To field.**

   If your recipient is listed in your Contacts on your iPod touch, tap the circled plus (+) sign in the To field (see Figure 11-4) and choose a contact to add the contact's e-mail address to the To field. You can repeat this process to add multiple e-mail addresses to the To field from your contacts.

   If your recipient isn't listed in your Contacts or if you don't know whether the recipient is listed, tap the To field entry and use the keyboard to type one or more e-mail addresses (and use a comma to separate each address). As you type an e-mail address, e-mail addresses that match from your Contacts list appear below. Tap one to add it to the To field.

5. **(Optional) Add more addresses to the Cc or Bcc fields.**

   You can add e-mail addresses to the Cc (carbon copy) and Bcc (blind carbon copy) fields to copy others. While Cc addresses appear on messages received by recipients indicating that they were copied on the message, Bcc addresses don't appear on messages received by recipients — they're like stealth readers. Tap the Cc/Bcc letters to expand the message to include the Cc and Bcc fields; then enter addresses the same way you do in Step 4.

6. **(Optional) Change the From address.**

   You can change the e-mail address for the sender to one of your e-mail accounts. The default e-mail account for sending e-mail is already selected; tap the From letters to display a pop-up menu of e-mail accounts and then tap an e-mail account to use as the sender's account.

7. **Enter the e-mail subject.**

   Tap the Subject entry field (refer to Figure 11-4) to type a subject with the keyboard; then tap underneath the Subject field to type a message. Press Return on the keyboard when you're finished.

8. **Tap Send in the upper-right corner of the display (refer to Figure 11-4) to send the message.**

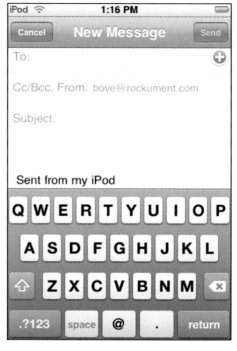

Figure 11-4: The New Message screen for multiple accounts.

You can also forward and reply to any message you receive. Open the message and tap the curled left-arrow button that appears in the bottom-left side of the message display. Then tap Reply to reply to the sender of the message, Reply All to reply to all of the recipients as well as the sender (if there are other recipients), or Forward to forward the message to someone else (or Cancel to go back to the message). The New Message screen appears with the onscreen keyboard so that you can type your reply or add a message to the one you're forwarding. Tap Send to send the reply or forwarded message.

When you reply to a message, files or images attached to the initial message aren't sent with the reply. When you tap Forward to forward a message, a pop-up menu with the Include or Don't Include buttons appears for a message with an attachment. Tap Include to include the attachment in the forwarded message, or Don't Include to forward the message without the attachment.

To save a message as a draft so you can work on it later, start typing the message as described in the preceding steps, but before tapping Send, tap Cancel in the upper-left corner of the display (refer to Figure 11-4). Then, from the menu that appears, tap Save to save the message in your Drafts mailbox or tap Don't Save to discard the message (or Cancel to go back to typing the message). You can find the saved message in the Drafts mailbox of the same e-mail account. Tap the message to add to it or change it and then send it.

To send a photo in a message, tap the Photos icon on the Home screen and choose a photo for viewing, as described in Chapter 9.

Message Settings and Sending Options

To change your e-mail message settings and sending options, choose Settings⇨Mail, Contacts, Calendars from the Home screen. In the Mail, Contacts, Calendars settings screen that appears, use your finger to scroll down to the Mail section to change your e-mail message settings and sending options, as shown in Figure 11-5.

In the Mail section, you can change global settings for messages in all accounts. To set the number of messages you can see at once in a mailbox, tap Show and then choose a setting. You can choose to see the most recent 25, 50, 75, 100, or 200 messages. (To down-load additional messages when you're in Mail, scroll to the bottom of your Inbox and tap Download More.)

TIP

If you think you have shaky fingers and might delete a message by mistake, you can set Mail to confirm that you want to delete a message first before deleting. Tap the Off button to turn on the Ask Before Deleting option. (Tap it again to turn it off.) If Ask Before Deleting is on, Mail warns you first when you delete a message, and you have to tap Delete to confirm the deletion.

What you see is what you got

You can also set how many lines of each message are previewed in the message list headers. Choose Preview (refer to Figure 11-5) and then choose to see any amount from zero to five lines of each message. To set a minimum font size for messages, tap Minimum Font Size and then choose Small, Medium, Large, Extra Large, or Giant.

iPod 🛜	5:17 PM	🔋
Settings	**Mail, Contacts, Calen...**	

Show	50 Recent Messages >
Preview	2 Lines >
Minimum Font Size	Medium >
Show To/Cc Label	OFF
Ask Before Deleting	OFF
Load Remote Images	OFF
Always Bcc Myself	OFF
Signature	Sent from my iPod >
Default Account	Tony on Mobi... >

Figure 11-5: The Mail section of Mail, Contacts, and Calendars settings.

If you want to see all the images in your e-mails and don't mind waiting for the images to download, turn on the Load Remote Images option. If you leave it off, your messages appear faster, but you have to touch each image icon to download and see it.

If you care about whether a message was sent directly to you or whether you were sent it as a Cc copy (which still might make it important, but at least you know), you can set whether Mail shows the To and Cc labels in message lists. Tap the Off button for the Show To/Cc Label option to turn it on. (Tap it again to turn it off.) If Show To/Cc Label is on, you see To or Cc in the list next to each message.

Return to sender, address unknown

For those who are obsessive about making sure e-mails are sent — and you know who you are — Mail can send you a copy of every message you send. Tap the Off button to turn on the Always Bcc Myself option. (Tap it again to turn it off.) The Bcc refers to *blind carbon copy,* and it means that your message is sent and copied back to you without your e-mail address appearing in the recipient's list.

You can add a *signature* to your messages that can include any text — not your real, handwritten scrawl but rather a listing of your name, title, phone number, favorite quote, or all of these — to personalize your e-mails. Tap Signature (refer to Figure 11-5) and then type a signature with the onscreen keyboard. The signature remains in effect for all future e-mails sent from your iPod touch.

To set the default e-mail account for sending messages, tap Default Account (refer to Figure 11-5) and then choose an e-mail account. Your iPod touch will use this account whenever you start the process of sending a message from another application, such as sending a photo from Photos or tapping the e-mail address of a business in Maps.

For details on synchronizing e-mail accounts automatically from iTunes or MobileMe, as well as for setting up an account, changing account settings, and deleting accounts manually on your iPod touch, see Chapter 6.

If Not Push, Then Fetch

The Push and Fetch options control how your iPod touch receives e-mail. You can set these options for each account and for all accounts.

MobileMe, Microsoft Exchange, and Yahoo! Mail e-mail accounts can *push* messages *to* your iPod touch so that they arrive immediately after arriving at the account's e-mail server. Other types of accounts *fetch* messages *from* the account's e-mail server — either on a time schedule or manually. (If manually, you select the account before your iPod touch retrieves the email.) Push accounts (such as MobileMe email) can be set to either push or fetch.

You can turn the Push feature on or off as you please. Keeping it on uses more battery power because the iPod touch receives messages immediately — whenever it's connected to Wi-Fi. When you turn the Push feature off, push accounts fetch the e-mail instead, and you can set the timetable for fetching, or set fetching to manual.

For optimal battery life, turn Push off and set Fetch to Manually so that fetching occurs only when you tap the e-mail account to read or send e-mail. Pushing e-mail as it arrives, or fetching e-mail often, uses up a considerable amount of battery power; doing both drains the battery even more quickly.

To turn Push on or off, choose Settings⇨Mail, Contacts, Calendars from the Home screen and tap Fetch New Data. The Fetch New Data screen appears, as shown in Figure 11-6. Tap the On button for Push to turn it off (and vice versa).

You can set a timetable for fetching e-mail automatically. Choose a time interval in the Fetch New Data screen (see Figure 11-6) — pick Every 15 Minutes, Every 30 Minutes, or Hourly. You can also pick Manually so that the iPod touch fetches only when you tap the e-mail account to read or send e-mail.

You can also set Push or Fetch settings for individual accounts. Scroll the Fetch New Data screen to the bottom and touch Advanced. The Advanced screen appears, as shown in Figure 11-7. Each account in the list shows Push or Fetch, depending on whether the account offers push email or not. Tap the account to change its settings separately.

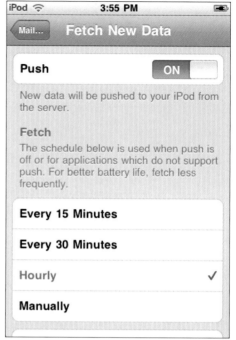

Figure 11-6: Push and Fetch settings that affect all accounts.

Figure 11-7: Choose an account (left) and set Push and Fetch settings for it (right).

You can set a push account to use the Fetch settings in the Fetch New Data screen instead. You can also set a fetch account to use the Fetch New Data screen settings, or to fetch only manually.

Setting Push to Off or setting Fetch to Manually in the Fetch New Data screen overrides the individual account settings.

12

Earth, Wind, and Finance

*Y*our iPod touch can find almost anything on Earth, even itself, and show the location on a map or satellite picture. And although you can't harness the forces of nature, or even the influences that drive Wall Street, you can use your iPod touch to make better guesses about the weather and the stock market.

This chapter describes how to use the Maps app to find any location on Earth and obtain driving directions — without having to ask someone out on the street. Your iPod touch offers Location Services to nail down the unit's physical location, and it offers that information to the Maps app and any other app that needs it, so that you can instantly find out where you are in the world.

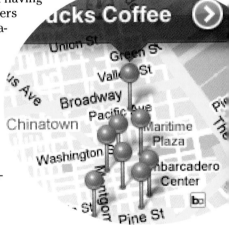

I also describe how to use the Weather and Stocks apps. Your iPod touch can connect to the Internet over Wi-Fi to get real-time information about the weather and the stock market. You can personalize the Stocks app to reflect your exact portfolio, and you can add cities to the Weather app to check conditions before you travel to them.

Tapping Your Maps

I once had to find my way to a meeting on a university campus that I was already late for, and, after driving endlessly around the campus looking for the proper entranceway, I tapped the Maps icon on my iPod touch and was able to immediately look up the location, see a map of it, and get directions. The Maps app is that good — most paper maps aren't even accurate for city streets, let alone campus driveways. (And yes, I pulled over to the curb first for safety.)

The Maps app provides street maps, satellite photos, and hybrid street-satellite views of locations all over the world. It also offers detailed driving directions from any location to just about any other location — unless you can't get there from here.

Where are you?

To use Maps, tap the Maps icon on the Home screen. The Maps app appears, as shown in Figure 12-1, ready for zooming, scrolling, or searching specific locations.

You can zoom in to the map by double-tapping the map with one finger or unpinching with your fingers. To zoom out, pinch with your fingers or double-tap with two fingers. You can also drag the map to pan around it and see more areas.

To find out where you are, tap the Compass icon in the bottom-left corner of the map screen. (See Figure 12-1.) A dialog appears, asking whether Maps can use your current location; tap OK to use it. The map then changes to show your general location with a compass-like circle representing your approximate physical location, as shown in Figure 12-2.

This circle continues to shrink as Maps retrieves more accurate information. Maps figures out where you are by using information from some local Wi-Fi networks (if you have Wi-Fi turned on). The more accurate the available information, the smaller the circle on the map becomes.

Search entry   Bookmarks

Compass   Underneath

Figure 12-1: The Maps app initial screen.

Figure 12-2: The compass shows your current location and shrinks to pinpoint it more accurately.

Searching locations

To find a location and see a map, tap the Maps icon on the Home screen and then tap the Search field at the top of the Maps screen that appears. The onscreen keyboard appears so that you can enter information.

You can find any location by its address or closest landmark, or you can find the physical address of a friend: Type the name of someone in your contacts list, or an address, an intersection, the name of a landmark or of a general area, or a zip code.

For example, to search for a friend, start typing the person's name. If the letters you type match any names with street addresses in your Contacts list, Maps offers them up as suggestions, as shown in Figure 12-3. Tap a suggested name to look up that person's home or business address.

Figure 12-3: Find the location of a friend in your Contacts.

You can also use the Contacts app to view your contacts list and then tap a contact's address to see that person's address in Maps.

To search for a landmark, an intersection, a zip code, or a type of business, type as much as you know into the Search field — such as **94111 pizza** for a pizza shop in the 94111 zip code. If the landmark is well known, type its name, as shown in Figure 12-4. Then tap the Search key in the onscreen keyboard. A red pin appears to mark the location you've searched for on the map (see Figure 12-4, right side), with a label showing the address.

To clear the entry from the Search field quickly, tap the *x* on the right side of the field. You can then type a new search term.

Figure 12-4: Type a search term and tap the Search button (left) to see the location (right).

If you search for the name of a business or type of business *after* searching for your own location, as I do in Figure 12-5, Maps is smart enough to locate the closest ones. Multiple pins appear on the map, showing the location of each business.

Pinpointing the spot

Red pins mark the locations you've searched for on the map (refer to Figure 12-4 and Figure 12-5, right side), and each has a label (such as "Graceland" or "Starbucks"). You can also drop your own pin on the map to pinpoint an exact spot so that you can bookmark it. The pin you drop is purple until you bookmark it and give it a name. (See "Bookmarking the spot," later in this chapter.)

Figure 12-5: From your location, type the name of a popular business (left) to see its nearest locations (right).

To drop your own pin, follow these steps:

1. **Drag the map to pan around and see more areas and zoom in to the location you want to pinpoint by double-tapping the map with one finger or unpinching with your fingers.**

2. **After finding the right location, tap the Underneath button — the curled page icon in the bottom-right corner (refer to Figure 12-1).**

   You see a menu underneath the map, as shown in Figure 12-6 (left side).

3. **Tap the Drop Pin button in the menu.**

   A purple pin appears on the map with the label `Drag To Move Pin` (see Figure 12-6, center).

4. **Touch the pin and drag it on the map to put it where you want it.**

   You can unpinch the map to zoom in further; drag the pin to a precise point, such as an intersection; pinch to zoom out; and drag to pan the map to see other areas.

5. **Tap the circled right arrow on the right side of the label to set the pin's location and to see the Info screen (see Figure 12-6, right side). Then pick what you want to do next.**

   From the Info screen, you can

   - Get directions to or from the location (as I describe in "Getting directions" in this chapter).

   - Remove the pin.

   - Add the pin to your bookmarks (as I describe in the next section).

   After adding the pin to your bookmarks, it changes from purple to red. You can add as many pins as you want to your map and save them as bookmarks.

To see a list of all pinpointed places on your map, tap the Underneath button and tap List. You can then tap any location in the list to select that specific pin and its label.

Figure 12-6: Drop a pin (left) to pinpoint a location (center) and then open the Info screen (right).

Bookmarking the spot

It makes sense to bookmark your home, your zip code (to make it easy to find businesses in your area), your office, and any other locations you visit often. After you've saved bookmarks, you can go back to any location by tapping the Bookmarks icon in the Search field (refer to Figure 12-1) to bring up a list of bookmarked locations and then tapping a location.

To bookmark a location after searching for it or dropping a pin, tap the circled right arrow on the right side of the pin's label to see the Info screen, as shown in Figure 12-7 (left side). You can then mark the spot with a bookmark that includes a name and description or do other things such as get directions. (See the "Getting directions" section in this chapter.)

Tap the Add to Bookmarks button on the Info screen, which brings up the onscreen keyboard so that you can type a name for the location, as shown in Figure 12-7 (right side). Tap Save in the upper-right corner of the Add Bookmark screen to save the bookmark (or Cancel to cancel the bookmark). Tap Map in the upper-left corner of the Info screen to go back to the map.

Figure 12-7: The Info screen for the location (left) for saving a bookmark (right).

You can also touch the pin or its label and then tap Directions To Here or Directions From Here (refer to Figure 12-7, left side) to get directions. (See the later section, "Getting directions.")

To go directly to a bookmarked location, tap the Bookmarks icon in the Search field (refer to Figure 12-1) and then tap a location, or tap the Done button in the upper-right corner to return to the map.

The Bookmarks icon in the Search field also offers a list of the recently searched locations as well as access to your Contacts list. Tap the Bookmarks icon and then tap the Recents button at the bottom of the screen to see a list of recent locations found on the map. Tap the Contacts button next to Recents to view your Contacts and select one to see that person's address on the map. Tap the Done button in the upper-right corner to return to the map.

A bird's-eye view

Do you want to see what the location looks like? You can change the view of the location to show a satellite image (if available), a hybrid of street view and satellite, or a list of bookmarked locations. Tap the Underneath button — the curled page icon in the bottom-right corner (refer to Figure 12-1) — to see a menu underneath the map. Then tap Satellite to view a satellite image of the site, as shown in Figure 12-8. You can zoom in to the image the same way you zoom in to the map.

Figure 12-8: Choose Satellite view (left) to see a satellite image of the location (center); choose Hybrid for a satellite-map view (right).

You can also view a hybrid of satellite image and street map — tap the Underneath button and then tap Hybrid in the menu underneath the map.

Getting directions

To get driving directions from one location to another, you first need to search for or pinpoint a location, as described in the previous section, and then tap Directions at the bottom of the map screen (refer to Figure 12-4, right side).

For example, if you want to get directions from your current location to a bookmarked location, first find your physical location on the map by tapping the compass icon in the bottom-left corner of the map screen (refer to Figure 12-2). Then tap Directions, and in the Directions screen that appears, your current location already occupies the Start field. Tap the Bookmarks icon in the End field and select a bookmarked location for the End field.

You can also tap a pin on a map to see the Info screen for that location, as shown in Figure 12-9, and then tap Directions To Here or Directions From Here to get directions. The Directions screen appears, with the first location selected as either the Start or End. For example, in Figure 12-9, I tapped Directions To Here, which automatically placed the location in the End field.

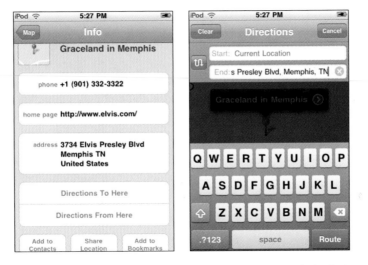

Figure 12-9: Tap Directions To Here (left) to put the location in the End field (right).

You can also type entries or select bookmarks for both the Start and End fields by tapping those fields and using the onscreen keyboard (refer to Figure 12-9, right side).

You can switch the entry for Start to End (or vice versa) by tapping the looped arrow button to the left of the Start and End fields. Using this button, you can get directions one way; then tap the button to reverse the Start and End fields to get directions for the way back.

After setting your Start and End locations, tap Route in the bottom-right corner of the onscreen keyboard (refer to Figure 12-9, right side) to mark the route on the map. Alternatively, you can tap Clear in the upper-left corner to reenter your Start and End fields, or Cancel in the upper-right corner to cancel getting directions.

As shown in Figure 12-10, the route on the map in the Overview screen is purple, with pins marking the start and end locations. Tap the car icon at the top of the Overview screen to see driving directions and the approximate driving time. If traffic data is available, the driving time is adjusted accordingly, but don't expect miracles — the information depends on data collected and services provided by third parties, not by Apple, and traffic patterns change. You can also tap the bus icon to see public transit directions, or tap the walking man icon to see walking directions.

Figure 12-10: Tap Start to see the route (left) step by step from beginning to end (right).

Digging into Google Earth

Find the source of the Nile River and follow it all the way to the great pyramids in Egypt (which you can see in the fourth figure). Or just take a peek in your neighbor's backyard or the streets where I live (the second figure with blue dot). Google Earth, available for free for desktop computers, lets you fly anywhere on Earth to view satellite imagery, maps, terrain, 3D buildings, from galaxies in outer space to the canyons and mystery spots of the ocean.

The Google Earth app for the iPod touch displays the same imagery and offers the same navigational capabilities as the desktop version, and it includes layers with geo-located Wikipedia articles and Panoramio photos with details (as shown in the third figure), as well as map labels and borders. With the Search Near Me function, query results are not only geo-located within Google Earth, but also are automatically relevant to your location — search for "pizza" while in San Francisco, and it shows a collection of San Francisco pizza restaurants. The Auto tilt feature uses the iPod touch built-in accelerometer to change your view in Google Earth when you tilt the iPod touch — you can tilt at an angle to see a skyline view of a location or tilt it all the way to see the sky itself. You can even track your movements on the planet: Tap the Location button to see a blue dot corresponding to your location (see the second figure with blue dot), and as your location changes, the dot and your view in Google Earth are updated accordingly.

To view directions one step at a time on the map, tap Start in the upper-right corner of the Overview screen (refer to Figure 12-10, left side) to see the first leg of the journey. Then tap the right-arrow button in the upper-right corner of the first leg's screen to see the next stretch (refer to Figure 12-10, right side). You can also tap the left-arrow button in any of the step-by-step directions to go back a step. The Maps application graciously walks you through your entire journey.

To view all the legs of your journey in a list, tap the Underneath icon in the lower-right corner of the display, and tap List. Then tap any location in the list to see a map showing that leg of the trip.

To see your most recent set of directions, tap the Bookmarks icon in the Search field and tap Recents at the bottom of the Bookmarks screen to change it to the Recents screen. If you close Maps and return to it later, your directions appear automatically. Tap the Done button in the upper-right corner to return to the map.

You can also get travel directions in advance (using Google Maps on your computer) and then transfer them to your iPod touch by e-mail. You can then open the e-mail on your iPod touch and tap the Google Maps embedded link — Maps opens automatically to show you the directions. As you open more e-mails and tap more links, your directions are remembered in Maps on your iPod touch in the Recents screen.

Riding on the Storm

The Weather app provided with your iPod touch looks up the current temperature and weather conditions, and it provides a six-day forecast for any city of your choice. (Of course, your iPod touch needs to be connected to Wi-Fi and the Internet for the Weather app to work.) Weather isn't the only app that does this — you can try other apps such as The Weather Channel, WeatherBug, or AccuWeather (all free).

To use Weather, tap the Weather icon on the Home screen. In daytime, the weather screen is light blue, and at night it's dark purple. What makes Weather useful is your ability to add your own cities — as many as you need — so that you can look up the weather in multiple locations instantly.

To add a city, follow these steps:

1. **Tap the *i* button in the lower-right corner of the weather display for your city, as shown in Figure 12-11 (left side).**

Figure 12-11: Tap the *i* button in Weather (left) to view the list of cities (center) and to add another city (right).

2. **Tap the plus (+) sign in the upper-left corner of the Weather screen (Figure 12-11, center).**

   A location field appears with the onscreen keyboard (Figure 12-11, right side).

3. **Enter the city's name or zip code — as you type, suggestions appear below in a list.**

4. **Choose one of the suggestions or continue typing the city name or zip code and then tap Search.**

   The city you chose appears in the list of cities in the Weather screen, with a circled minus (–) sign next to it on the left and three horizontal gray bars on the right, as shown in Figure 12-12 (left side).

   At this point, you can add more cities by tapping the plus (+) sign in the upper-left corner again. You can also reorder the list of cities by dragging the three gray bars next to a city to a new place in the list, as shown in Figure 12-12 (right side).

To delete a city, tap the circled minus sign next to the city name to show the Delete button and then tap the Delete button (or tap the circled minus sign again to leave it alone).

Tap the Done button in the top-right corner of the Weather screen to finish adding cities and see the weather display for your city.

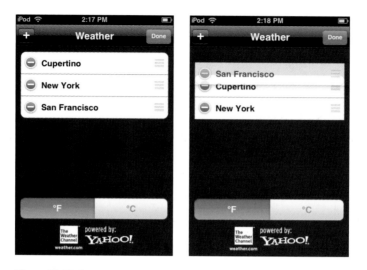

Figure 12-12: Reorder the list of cities in Weather (left) by dragging the three gray horizontal bars for the city (right).

To switch from one city to the next, flick your finger over the city weather display horizontally or tap the tiny white buttons at the bottom of the city weather display (refer to Figure 12-11, left side).

Tapping Your Moneymaker

You can check your financial stocks, funds, and indexes with your iPod touch as long as it's connected to Wi-Fi and the Internet. (Whether the news is good or bad, you can quickly e-mail your broker — see Chapter 11.)

Tap the Stocks icon on the Home screen. The Stocks app displays a few stocks and indexes you may be interested in (such as Apple and Google), and it shows updated quotes if the iPod touch is connected to the Internet (although quotes may be delayed by up to 20 minutes). Scroll the Stocks list by dragging or flicking it with your finger.

Swipe the lower section of the Stocks screen to see a summary, a graph (as shown in Figure 12-13, left side), or the latest news. To see a current graph of the stock, swipe the lower section to the center and then tap the 1d (one day), 1w (one week), 1m (one month), 3m (three months), 6m (six months), 1y (one year), or 2y (two years) buttons above the graph in the stock reader. Tap the change number next to each stock to switch to show the percentage change, the market cap, or the change in price.

Of course, you'll want to add your portfolio to Stocks. To add a stock, index, or fund to watch, here's what you do:

1. **Tap the *i* button in the lower-right corner of the stock reader, as shown in Figure 12-13 (left side).**

2. **Tap the plus (+) sign in the upper-left corner of the Stocks screen (Figure 12-13, center).**

   The Add Stock field appears with the onscreen keyboard (Figure 12-13, right side).

3. **Enter the stock symbol or company name (or index or fund name).**

   As you type, suggestions appear below in a list.

4. **Choose one of the suggestions or continue typing the symbol or name and then touch Search.**

   The stock, fund, or index you chose appears in the list in the Stocks screen, with a circled minus (–) sign next to it on the left, and three horizontal gray bars on the right, as shown in Figure 12-14.

   At this point, if you want to add more stocks, funds, or indexes, tap the plus (+) sign in the upper-left corner again. To reorder a list of stocks, drag the three gray bars next to a stock to a new place in the list.

To delete a stock, tap the circled minus sign next to the stock name to show the Delete button and then tap the Delete button (or tap the circled minus sign again to leave it alone).

Tap the Done button in the top-right corner of the Stocks screen to finish adding stocks and see the stock reader.

Figure 12-13: Touch the *i* button in Stocks (left) to view the list (center) and to add another stock, fund, or index (right).

Figure 12-14: Reorder the list in Stocks (left) by dragging the three gray horizontal bars for the stock, fund, or index (right).

Part V
Staying in Touch and Up-to-Date

The 5th Wave   By Rich Tennant

"You ever notice how much more streaming media there is than there used to be?"

By now you should be accustomed to using your iPod touch like a small computer — and that's just what it is, a computer in your pocket that runs apps from the App Store. Some of these apps are just as powerful as the ones on your computer, especially ones that connect you to your social world.

Chapter 13 puts you in contact with your contacts, helps you manage your calendar, and connects you with the most popular social networks on the planet — Facebook, MySpace, and Twitter.

I saved the unfunny stuff for Chapter 14: how to keep your iPod touch software up-to-date, how to reset the software and your settings, and how to restore your iPod touch to pristine factory condition.

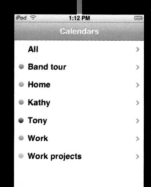

A Day in the Social Life

In This Chapter

▶ Checking your calendar and entering events

▶ Entering and sorting your contacts

▶ Connecting to social networks like Facebook and MySpace

As John Lennon once sang, "Life is what happens to you when you're busy making other plans." And while life happens to you in real time, you can consult your iPod touch Calendar app to view your appointments, change them, and make new ones. One of the major benefits of using an iPod touch is the onscreen keyboard, which you can use to enter text, such as calendar entries, as I describe in this chapter.

In this chapter, I also demonstrate how to look up contact names, addresses, and phone numbers with your iPod touch, change contact information, and add new contacts. Any changes you make to calendars and contacts are synchronized with your desktop applications (as I describe in Chapter 6).

To socialize and stay in contact with friends, relatives, and associates, you can use social networks such as Facebook and MySpace to share photos, thoughts, links, and profile information. The App Store offers social networking apps that link you directly to these networks, and to messaging sites such as Twitter. You'll find all this and more in this chapter on your social life with iPod touch.

Silverstein was tagged
sum.

sta Rica by Josh Silv

Checking Your Calendar

The Calendar app isn't just for looking up dates (though it's quite good at that). If you see a blank calendar, it means you need to synchronize your iPod touch with your calendar files from iCal (Mac) or Outlook (Windows), as I describe in Chapter 6.

Tap the Calendar icon on the Home screen. Here's what happens:

✔ **If this is your first visit to the Calendar app and you've synchronized multiple calendars to your iPod touch,** a list of your calendars appears (see Figure 13-1, left side). Tap All at the top to view all calendars merged into one or tap a specific calendar to see only that calendar. The calendar appears in a monthly view by default (see Figure 13-1, right side).

✔ **If you opened Calendar before,** the app shows the calendar and view opened previously.

Tap any day to see the events on that day, which are displayed below the calendar view in a list.

Figure 13-1: The Calendar app's list of calendars (left) and monthly view (right).

Tap the List, Day, or Month buttons to change the calendar view to a list of events, a full day of scheduled appointments, or a month view, respectively. If you roam around from day to day or month to month, tap the Today button in the lower-left corner of the display to see the calendar for today.

A change is gonna come

Change happens, and you'll want to change your schedule or even add new events as you learn about them. Although you can enter appointments and events on your computer and sync them with your iPod touch, as I show you in Chapter 6, you can also enter and change appointments and events directly in your iPod touch and keep changes and additions synced with your computer.

To add an event, follow these steps:

1. **Open the Calendar app as described earlier.**

   The Calendar app opens (refer to Figure 13-1) — either the Calendar view appears, or if you have multiple calendars, the list of calendars appears — in which case you need to tap a calendar to use for the new event.

2. **Tap the plus (+) sign in the upper-right corner of the Calendar screen.**

   The Add Event screen appears, as shown in Figure 13-2 (left side).

3. **Tap the Title Location button and enter the event's title and location using the onscreen keyboard.**

   The Title and Location fields appear along with the onscreen keyboard, as shown in Figure 13-2 (right side).

Figure 13-2: Add an event in Calendar (left) and give it a title and location (right).

4. **Tap Save in the upper-right corner to save the entry (or Cancel in the upper-left corner to cancel the entry).**

   The Add Event screen appears again for selecting more options, as shown in Figure 13-3 (left side).

5. **Tap the Starts Ends button to enter the starting and ending times and dates.**

   The Start & End screen appears, as shown in Figure 13-3 (right side), with a slot-machine-style number wheel to select the date and time.

Figure 13-3: Tap Starts Ends (left) and enter starting and ending dates and times (right).

6. **Tap the Starts button and select the date and time or tap the Off button for All-Day to turn on the All-Day option.**

   Slide your finger up and down the slot-machine-style number wheel to select the date and time. If you turn on the All-Day option, the number wheel changes to show only dates; select a date for the all-day event and skip the next step.

7. **Tap the Ends button and select the date and time as you did in Step 6.**

8. **Tap Save in the upper-right corner to save the entry (or Cancel in the upper-left corner to cancel the entry).**

   The Add Event screen appears again for selecting more options (refer to Figure 13-3, left side).

9. **(Optional) Set the event to repeat by tapping Repeat and selecting a repeat time; then tap Save (or Cancel).**

   You can set the event to repeat every day, every week, every two weeks, every month, or every year (or none, to not repeat). After you tap Save or Cancel, the Add Event screen appears again for selecting more options.

10. **(Optional) Set an alert for a time before the event by tapping Alert and choosing an alert time; then tap Save (or Cancel).**

    You can set the alert to occur from five minutes to two days before the event. You can also set a second alert time in case you miss the first one. After you tap Save or Cancel, the Add Event screen appears again for selecting more options.

11. **(Optional) If you have multiple calendars synced with your iPod touch, you can change the calendar for the event by tapping Calendar and choosing a calendar.**

    The Calendars screen appears with a list of your calendars. Tap a calendar's name to choose it. After you tap Save or Cancel, the Add Event screen appears again for changing event options.

12. **(Optional) Enter notes about the event by tapping Notes and using the onscreen keyboard to type notes.**

    The Notes field appears along with the keyboard so that you can type your notes. After you tap Save or Cancel, the Add Event screen appears again for changing event options.

13. **Tap Done in the upper-right corner of the Add Event screen to save the event (or Cancel in the upper-left corner to cancel the event).**

    The new event now appears in your calendar in the lower portion of the Calendar screen when you select the day, as shown in Figure 13-4 (left side).

To edit an event, tap the event in the lower portion of the Calendar screen, and then tap Edit in the upper-right corner of the Event screen. The event information appears and is ready for editing or deleting, as shown in Figure 13-4 (right side). To edit the event information, follow Steps 3–13 in this section.

The Delete Event button appears only when you're editing an event. After tapping Delete Event, a warning appears to confirm the deletion — tap Delete Event again or tap Cancel. The Calendar screen appears.

Figure 13-4: Tap the event title (left) to edit or delete the event (right).

Yesterday's settings (and today's)

You can set alerts for meeting invitations and choose how many weeks of events to sync back to (to clear out old events). Choose Settings⇨Mail, Contacts, Calendars from the Home screen and then scroll the Mail, Contacts, Calendars settings screen to the Calendars section, as shown in Figure 13-5 (left side).

To set the option for how far back in time to sync your calendar events, tap Sync and choose a period of time (such as Events 2 Weeks Back).

If you have a Microsoft Exchange account set up with Calendars enabled, you can receive and respond to meeting invitations from others in your organization that also use Exchange. To set a sound as an alert for receiving a meeting invitation, tap the Off button for New Invitation Alerts to turn it on.

You can also turn time zone support on or off. When time zone support is on, event dates and times are displayed in the time zone of the city you selected. When time zone support is off, events are displayed in the time zone of your current location as determined by the network time. You might want to turn it on and select your home city so that dates and times are displayed as if you were in your home city, rather than where you actually are. For example, if you live in San Francisco and you're visiting New York, turning on Time Zone Support and selecting San Francisco keeps the dates and times in your calendars on San Francisco time. Otherwise, they would switch to New York time.

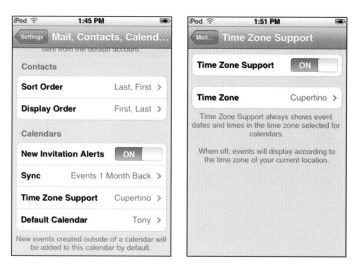

Figure 13-5: The Contacts and Calendars sections for settings (left) and the Time Zone setting (right).

To turn on time zone support, tap Time Zone Support, and on the Time Zone Support screen (refer to Figure 13-5, right side), tap Off to turn on Time Zone Support (or tap On to turn it off). Then tap Time Zone and enter the name of a major city. As you type, city names are suggested based on what you've typed. Select the city to return to the Time Zone Support screen and then tap the Mail button in the upper-left corner to return to the settings screen — or, if you're finished making changes, press the Home button to leave settings altogether and return to the Home screen.

You can set your iPod touch to play a beeping sound for your calendar alert. Choose Settings➪General➪Sounds and tap the Off button for Calendar Alerts to turn it on. (Tap it again to turn it off.)

Using Your Contacts

The bits of information that you're most likely to need on the road are people's names, addresses, and phone numbers. You can use the Contacts app on your iPod touch to store this information and keep it all in sync with your computer. (For sync info, see Chapter 6.)

To view contacts on an iPod touch, tap the Contacts icon on the Home screen. The All Contacts screen appears. If you've organized contacts into groups, you can tap the Groups button in the upper-left corner of the screen to show the Groups screen, and then tap a group to see just that group, or tap All Contacts to return to the All Contacts screen.

The contact list is sorted automatically in alphabetical order by last name (in bold) but displayed so that the first name comes first, as shown in Figure 13-6. Scroll the list of contacts with your finger or tap a letter of the alphabet along the right side to go directly to names that begin with that letter. Then tap a contact to see that person's info screen.

The contact's info screen shows all the information about reaching that contact. Tap an e-mail address to bring up the Mail app and send an e-mail to that contact. Tap a Web site address to load that page into Safari. Tap a physical address (with a street address) to bring up the Maps app and locate the contact on the map.

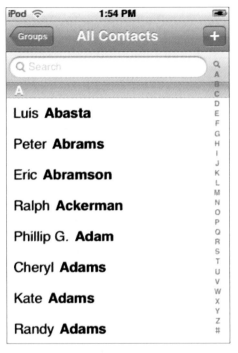

Figure 13-6: Scroll the alphabetical list or tap a letter along the right side.

Orders to sort and display

You can change which way the contacts sort so that you can look up people by their first names (which can be time-consuming with so many friends named Elvis). Choose Settings⇨Mail, Contacts, Calendars and then scroll the Mail, Contacts, Calendars settings screen to the Contacts section (refer to Figure 13-5, left side). Tap Sort Order and then tap one of these options:

- ✔ **First, Last:** Sorts the contact list by first name, followed by the last name, so that *Brian Jones* sorts under the letter *B* for *Brian* (after *Brian Auger* but before *Brian Wilson*).

- ✔ **Last, First:** Sorts the contacts by last name, followed by the first name, so that *Brian Jones* sorts under the letter *J* for *Jones*. (*Jones, Brian* appears after *Jones, Alice* but before *Jones, Norah*.)

You can also display contacts with their first names followed by their last names, or last names followed by first names, regardless of how you sort them. Choose Settings⇨Mail, Contacts, Calendars and then scroll the Mail, Contacts, Calendars settings screen to the Contacts section. Tap Display Order and then tap one of these options:

✔ **First Last:** Displays the contacts list by first name and then last name, as in *Paul McCartney.*

✔ **Last, First:** Displays the contacts list by last name followed by a comma and the first name, as in *McCartney, Paul.*

Soul searchin'

Can't remember the person's full name or last name? You can search for any part of a person's name in Contacts by tapping the Search entry field at the very top of the list of contacts. The Search entry field appears with the onscreen keyboard, as shown in Figure 13-7, and suggestions appear as you type.

Tap a suggested name to open the Contacts record for that person. You can then edit or delete the contact information.

Adding, editing, and deleting contacts

You meet people all the time, so why not enter their information immediately? You can enter new contacts, edit existing contacts, and even delete contacts directly on your iPod touch, and keep your contacts in sync with your computer. (For sync info, see Chapter 6.)

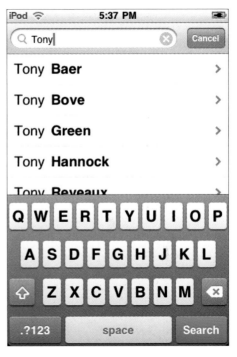

Figure 13-7: Search for a contact by typing part of a name.

To add a contact, follow these steps:

1. **Tap the Contacts icon on the Home screen.**

2. **Tap the plus (+) sign in the upper-right corner of the Contacts display.**

   The New Contact screen appears, as shown in Figure 13-8 (left side).

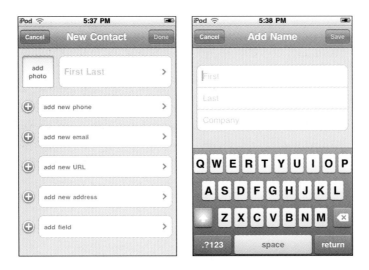

Figure 13-8: Add a new contact (left) and enter the contact's name (right).

3. **Tap the First Last button and enter the contact's first and last name, as well as the company name, using the onscreen keyboard.**

   The First, Last, and Company fields appear in the Add Name screen (see Figure 13-8, right side) along with the keyboard.

4. **Tap Save in the upper-right corner of the Add Name screen to save the name (or Cancel in the upper-left corner to cancel the name).**

   The New Contact screen appears again for selecting more options (refer to Figure 13-8, left side).

5. **Tap the Add New Phone button and enter the phone number and label for the number.**

   The Add Phone screen appears, as shown in Figure 13-9, with a numeric keyboard for typing the number. Tap the field under the number to select a label for the type of phone (mobile, home, work, main, home fax, and so on).

Figure 13-9: Enter the contact's phone number.

To enter a pause in a phone number (sometimes required for extensions or code numbers), tap the +*# button and tap Pause, which inserts a comma representing the pause. Each pause lasts two seconds; you can enter as many as you need.

6. **Tap Save in the upper-right corner of the Add Phone screen to save the phone number (or Cancel in the upper-left corner to cancel the entry).**

   The New Contact screen appears again for adding more information.

7. **Tap the Add New Email button to add an e-mail address using the onscreen keyboard and select a label for the type of e-mail address.**

   The Add Email screen appears with a field to enter the information, a button to set the label describing it, and the onscreen keyboard.

8. **Tap Save in the upper-right corner to save the entry (or Cancel in the upper-left corner to cancel the entry).**

   The New Contact screen appears again for adding more information.

9. **(Optional) Repeat Steps 7 and 8 with the Add New URL button to add a new URL (Web site address) for the contact.**

10. **Tap Add New Address on the New Contact screen, and add street (or P.O. Box) information, city, state, zip code, and country.**

    The keyboard appears with two entry fields for Street and one each for City, State, and Zip. Tap the country button to set the country, and the label button (set to home) for the type of address.

11. **Tap Save in the upper-right corner to save the address (or Cancel in the upper-left corner to cancel it).**

    The New Contact screen appears again for adding more information.

12. **(Optional) Tap Add Field to add more fields to the contact. When you're done, tap Save (or Cancel)**

    You can add a prefix, middle name, suffix, phonetic first and last names, nickname, job title, department, birthday, date, or note. Tap each field, and use the keyboard to type in the information. Tapping Save or Cancel returns you to the New Contact screen.

13. **(Optional) Add a photo.**

    To add a photo, tap Add Photo in the upper-left corner of the New Contact screen. A pop-up menu appears for you to tap Choose Existing Photo (or Cancel). You're taken immediately to the Photos app, where you can tap a photo album and then tap a photo. Finally, tap Set Photo (or Cancel).

14. **Tap Save in the upper-right corner of the New Contact screen to save the contact information (or Cancel in the upper-left corner to cancel the contact information).**

Instant voice and text messaging

The iPhone gets all the glory for its communicating abilities with its phone and SMS text messaging services provided by the service carrier (AT&T in the U.S.), but the iPod touch is no slouch in this department — in fact, the iPod touch can make you carrier-free. All you need is a Wi-Fi connection that accesses the Internet.

Skype is a service that lets you make phone calls over the Internet. Calls to other Skype users are free, but calls to other landlines and mobile phones require some money on your part. The Skype for iPhone app (free) works on the iPod touch to give you phone service and instant text messages to anyone else on Skype. All you need is a Wi-Fi connection and a microphone for your iPod touch (for voice calls). You can use the Apple In-Ear Headphones with Remote and Mic (available in the Apple Store) or products from other companies, such as V-MODA Vibe II with Microphone Headphone/Headset for iPhone/iPod, or TouchMic Handsfree Lapel Microphone and Adapter, which adds a microphone and volume control to any regular headset.

If all you need is instant messaging, try the AOL Instant Messenger (AIM) app, which is popular in the U.S. You can send and receive instant messages on your iPod touch, view your buddy list, and rearrange the entries in groups or separate them as favorites. If you're using a lot of different chat clients, the IM+ app may be a better choice — it supports AIM, Yahoo! Messenger, MSN, Google Talk, Jabber, ICQ and MySpace. Palringo is another excellent multifunctional instant messaging app that supports MSN, Yahoo! Messenger, AIM, Gadu-Gadu, ICQ, Jabber, Google Talk, and iChat.

If you're looking for an iPod touch app that lets you chat with Yahoo! Messenger folks and also connects with various other social networks, check out the oneConnect! app, which lets you keep an eye on your Facebook, Flickr, Last.fm, Twitter, Bebo, Dopplr, MySpace and YouTube accounts. There are even a few social networks set up specifically for iPhone and iPod touch users — for example, WhosHere (see figure) is a social proximity application that connects you with people who are nearby or anywhere in the world. You can send unlimited, free text and image messages to other WhosHere participants.

To edit a contact, tap the contact to see the contact's Info screen, then tap Edit in the upper-right corner of the Info screen to show the circled minus (–) sign and plus (+) sign buttons.

You can edit or delete any information for a contact while leaving the rest of the information intact. Tap any field to edit the information in that field. Tap the circled minus (–) sign next to the information to reveal a Delete button;

tap the Delete button to delete the information, or tap the circled minus sign again to leave it alone.

To change a photo, tap the existing photo in the upper-left corner of the Info screen. A pop-up menu appears for you to tap Choose Photo, Edit Photo, Delete Photo, or Cancel. Tap Choose Photo to choose a new photo as described in Step 13 earlier. To move or scale the photo, Tap Edit Photo to show the Move and Scale screen. Then pinch the image with your fingers to zoom out or unpinch to zoom in, and drag the image with your finger to show only a portion of it. Tap the Set Photo button in the bottom-right corner of the Move and Scale screen to save the edited image (or touch Cancel). You return again to the Info screen.

Tap Done in the upper-right corner of the Info screen to finish editing and return to the contact information.

To delete a contact entirely, tap Edit, scroll down to the bottom and then tap Delete Contact. Remember, if you do this, the contact will also be deleted from your contact list on your computer when you sync your iPod touch.

Recording Voice Memos

The Voice Memos app lets you record audio through an external microphone (such as the Apple In-Ear Headphones with Remote and Mic). You can then send recordings to others by e-mail, or sync them back to your computer's iTunes library. After syncing with iTunes (as I describe in Chapter 5), the recordings appear in the music portion of your iTunes library in the Voice Memos playlist (created for you if you don't already have one).

To start recording, tap the Voice Memos app on the Home screen and then tap the red dot button on the left side of the VU meter on the microphone recording screen. (You can also press the center button on the control capsule of the Apple In-Ear Headphones to start recording.) The red dot changes to a Pause button, as shown in Figure 13-10 (left side), and the list button on the right side of the VU meter changes to a Stop button. Tap the Pause or Stop button to stop recording.

Tap the list button on the right side of the VU meter to see the Voice Memos screen with your list of recordings, as shown in Figure 13-10 (center). Select a recording, and you can then tap Share to send it by e-mail, or tap Delete to delete it. After tapping Share, tap Email Voice Memo to open a new e-mail with the recording (or tap Cancel). See Chapter 11 for details on sending an e-mail.

You can also tap the Play button on the left of the recording to play it, and tap the right arrow on the far right side of the recording to open the Info screen for that recording, as shown in Figure 13-10 (right side).

Figure 13-10: Record your voice (left), select a saved recording (center), and open the Info screen (right).

How can you specify what the recording is about, besides its date and time? You can assign a label to the recording by tapping the recording's information in the Info screen. A list of labels appears, including Interview, Lecture, and Memo, as well as Custom for setting your own label. Tap a label to assign the label and then tap Info in the top-left corner to return to the Info screen.

The Info screen also lets you trim the recording to be shorter — tap Trim Memo to view the playback time-line, as shown in Figure 13-11, and tap along the timeline to set a stop time. Then tap Trim Voice Memo (or Cancel to cancel).

Tap Voice Memos in the top-left corner of the Info screen to return to the Voice Memos screen, and tap Done in the top-right corner to return to the microphone recording screen.

Figure 13-11: Trim your voice recording before sharing it.

Socializing on Networks

Connecting socially over a digital network isn't new — I connected to friends way back in the pre-Internet dark ages by using exotic-sounding networks such as Usenet, bulletin board systems (BBS), The Source, CompuServe, the WELL (Whole Earth 'Lectronic Link), and EIES (Murray Turoff's server-based Electronic Information Exchange Service). What's new is that more sophisticated social networks have appeared and gone mainstream very quickly, with MySpace, Facebook, and Twitter leading the pack.

You can use your iPod touch to stay in touch with your connections on these and many other social networks — viewing and typing messages, chatting, uploading and sharing photos, joining groups, and so on. All you need is a Wi-Fi connection so you can hop onto the Internet.

You've got a Facebook friend

Facebook is the fastest-growing free-access social networking site as of this writing, with more than 200 million active users worldwide. If you're one of them (as I am), you already know that you can add friends, send them messages, and update your personal profile with photos, videos, links, and all sorts of Facebook widgets that extend the service's functions. Although you can do all this using a browser on your computer and using Safari on your iPod touch, the site itself is far too cumbersome for easy access on your iPod touch. What's needed is a "baby Facebook" on the iPod touch.

And that's exactly what Facebook for iPhone is: This app — which also runs on the iPod touch — lets you check your friends' status updates and photos, start a conversation in Facebook Chat, and upload images from your iPod touch.

After downloading the Facebook app (see Chapter 4 for details on downloading apps), tap the Facebook icon on the Home screen and then log in to your Facebook account, as shown in Figure 13-12 (left side). Your Facebook home screen appears, as shown in Figure 13-12 (right side), showing your news feed (top stories, status updates, and photos). If you have any notifications, a number appears on top of the Notifications tab (see Figure 13-12, right side).

After logging in, the Facebook app remembers your username and password so that you don't have to type them to log in again. (Of course, that means if anyone grabs your iPod touch they'll have access to your Facebook account — use a passcode to lock up your iPod touch, as I describe in Chapter 3, so that no one can use it without the passcode.) If you don't want the Facebook app to remember your login info, tap the profile icon to see your profile screen and then tap the Logout button in the upper-left corner of the profile screen.

Along the bottom of the Facebook screen are the Home icon for returning to the Home screen, the profile icon (with your first name) for showing your profile, the Friends icon to access a list of your Facebook friends, and the Inbox icon to check your messages. You can also tap Chat to chat directly with any of your friends who are online.

Figure 13-12: Log in to your Facebook account (left) to see your home news feed (right).

The Facebook app even lets you upload and share photos: Tap the profile icon to see your profile and then tap Add a Photo. You can then pick a photo from your iPod touch photo albums, tag the photo with a person's name, and type a caption. Tap Upload to upload the photo, which is placed in the Mobile Uploads section of your profile photos.

MySpace odyssey

So you want to be a MySpace cowboy or cowgirl? MySpace, owned by Fox Interactive Media, was the most popular mainstream social networking site until Facebook came along. Today, it's the number-two service, and it's still an awesomely huge network. MySpace focuses on music, movies, and TV shows — just about every band in the universe has a MySpace page, and it's easy to add music to your profile.

You can use Safari on your iPod touch to access MySpace, but like most social networks, the home page you see is far too cumbersome for easy access on your iPod touch. The MySpace Mobile for iPhone app is much easier to use and works fine on your iPod touch as long as you have a Wi-Fi connection. It lets you send and receive messages, check status updates and photos, stay up-to-date on bulletins, and upload images from your iPod touch.

 After downloading the MySpace app (see Chapter 4 for app downloading details), tap the MySpace icon on the Home screen and log in to your MySpace account, as shown in Figure 13-13 (left side). As you log in, you can turn on the Remember Me option so that after logging in, the MySpace app remembers your username and password so that you don't have to log in again.

After you log in, your MySpace Home screen appears, as shown in Figure 13-13 (right side), with menu selections for viewing and editing your profile, checking the status and mood messages from your friends, checking friend updates, adding comments, reading bulletins, reading blogs, and changing your settings.

Along the bottom of the MySpace screen are the Home icon for returning to the Home screen, the Mail icon to check your messages, the Requests icon to view and respond to requests, the Friends icon for a list of your MySpace friends, and the Photos icon to upload photos to your MySpace page. To add photos, tap the Photos icon to see the photos already on your MySpace page and then tap the Add Photos button. You can then pick a photo from your iPod touch photo albums.

Figure 13-13: Log in to your MySpace account (left) to see your Home screen (right).

Dedicated follower of Twitter

The most talked-about newcomer to the social network scene is Twitter, a free social messaging utility for staying connected with people in real time. With Twitter, you can post and receive messages that are 140 characters or less — called *tweets*. All public tweets are available to read on the public timeline, or you can read just the ones posted by the Twitter members you follow. You can post a tweet that can be read by all of your followers and by anyone reading the public tweets.

Members use Twitter to organize impromptu gatherings, carry on a group conversation, or just send a quick update to let people know what's going on. Companies use Twitter to announce products and carry on conversations with their customers. You can use Safari on your iPod touch to access Twitter, but there are alternatives that offer a better Twitter experience on your iPod touch.

 For example, you can use the Twitter for iPhone Web service (`http://twitterforiphone.com`) with your iPod touch to easily flip through all of your messages with the flick of a finger. Twitter for iPhone offers a menu, as shown in Figure 13-14 (left side), for checking recent posts, updating your status, sending direct messages and replies to others on Twitter, browsing friends, and adding new friends (called *followers*).

There are several iPod touch–compatible apps in the App Store for accessing Twitter, but my favorite as of this writing is Twitterific — the free version includes advertising (see Figure 13-14, right side), but a premium version is also available without ads. The free version of Twitterific does all the basic stuff you'd expect a Twitter client to do: You can read messages from people you follow, post messages of your own, and get alerted to private direct messages and public replies.

And wherever you go, "tweetness follows." Twitterific taps into the iPod touch's built-in location services so that, with your permission, it can let your followers know where you are and let you know when your followers are posting from a nearby location. You can set options for viewing messages, optimize the interface for left-handed operation, and use its own mini-browser to view linked Web pages without having to quit the app and run Safari. You can also copy a link to the last-opened Web page in Safari on your iPod touch into a tweet — a very useful trick if you like to include Web links with your tweets. Tweet dreams!

Figure 13-14: Twitter for iPhone Web service (left), and Twitterific (right).

Resetting, Updating, and Restoring

This no-nonsense chapter may not be fun, but it's necessary. Humans aren't perfect, and neither are the machines they make. If your iPod touch stops working as it should, or an app causes it to freeze up, you can turn to this chapter. You also find out how to reset your network settings and the keyboard dictionary.

This chapter also covers updating the firmware and software on your iPod touch. (*Firmware* is software encoded in hardware.) All software devices need to be updated now and then — it's a good thing, because new versions fix known bugs and add improvements.

Finally, I describe how to restore your iPod touch to its factory default condition. Restoring to factory condition is a drastic measure that erases any music or information on the iPod touch, but it usually solves a software glitch when nothing else does.

Powering Down and Resetting

Sometimes problems arise with electronics and software that can prevent an iPod touch from returning from an app or from turning on properly with all its content and playlists. If your iPod touch freezes while running an app, press and hold the Home button below the screen for at least six seconds, until the app quits. If the iPod touch still doesn't respond, turn it off by pressing the Sleep/Wake (On/Off) button on the top and then press the same button again to turn it back on.

If that doesn't work, press and hold the Sleep/Wake button on the top for a few seconds until a red slider that says `Slide to power off` appears on the screen. Slide the slider with your finger to turn off the iPod touch. Then press and hold the Sleep/Wake button until the Apple logo appears. The iPod touch starts up again.

Resetting your iPod touch system

You probably won't be too surprised to discover that, on the off chance your iPod touch gets confused or refuses to turn on, you can fix it by resetting it and restarting the system — just like computers and other iPods. Resetting does *not* restore the iPod touch to its original factory condition, nor does it erase anything — your content and settings remain intact.

To reset the iPod touch, press and hold the Sleep/Wake button and the Home button at the same time for at least ten seconds, until the Apple logo appears.

After resetting, everything should be back to normal, including your music and data files.

Resetting your settings

You can reset all or part of your iPod touch settings while leaving your content and personal information intact. To see your resetting options, choose Settings⇨General⇨Reset from the Home screen. The Reset screen appears, as shown in Figure 14-1.

You have several options for resetting:

- **Reset All Settings:** To return your iPod touch to its original condition with no preferences or settings while still keeping your content or your personal information (including contacts, calendars, and e-mail accounts) intact, tap Reset All Settings.

- **Erase All Content and Settings:** To erase *everything,* first connect the iPod touch to your computer or a power adapter and then tap Erase All Content and Settings. This operation can take hours! It wipes out everything by overwriting the data stored on the iPod touch. You can't use the iPod touch until it finishes. It may be easier and faster to do a full restore from iTunes, as I describe later in this chapter, in the section "Restoring your iPod touch."

✔ **Reset Network Settings:** You can reset your network settings so that your previously used networks are removed from the Wi-Fi list. This type of reset is useful if you can't find any other way to stop a Wi-Fi network from connecting automatically to your iPod touch — just tap Reset Network Settings, and you're automatically disconnected from any Wi-Fi network. (Wi-Fi is turned off and then back on.) For more details about choosing Wi-Fi networks, see Chapter 4.

✔ **Reset Keyboard Dictionary:** To reset the keyboard dictionary, tap Reset Keyboard Dictionary. This erases all words that have been added to the dictionary. (Words are added when you reject words suggested by the onscreen keyboard and type the word — see Chapter 2 for details.)

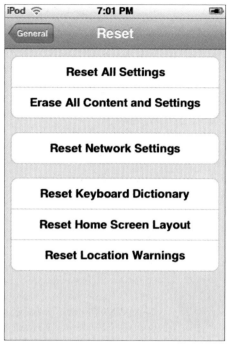

Figure 14-1: Options for resetting your iPod touch settings and clearing all content.

✔ **Reset Home Screen Layout:** If you rearranged the icons on your Home screen (as I describe in Chapter 2), you may want to set them back to their original positions. To reset your Home screen to the default arrangement, tap Reset Home Screen Layout.

✔ **Reset Location Warnings:** Location warnings are requests by apps to use the Location Services. The iPod touch stops displaying these warnings the second time you tap OK. If you want the iPod touch to start displaying the warnings again, tap Reset Location Warnings.

Updating Your iPod touch

You should always keep your iPod touch updated with new versions of the software that controls the device. iTunes automatically checks for updates of this software and lets you update your iPod touch without affecting the music or data stored on it.

Make sure that you use the newest version of iTunes. To check for the availability of an updated version for Windows, choose Help⇨Check for iTunes Updates.

If you use a Mac and you enabled the Software Update option in your System Preferences, Apple automatically informs you of updates to your Apple software for the Mac, including iTunes, Safari, iCal, and Address Book. All you need to do is select which updates to download and then click the Install button to download them. iTunes includes updates for all generations of iPods and can detect which iPod model you have.

Checking the software version

To determine which version of iPod software is installed on your iPod touch, choose Settings⇨General⇨About. Next to the word Version is information that describes the software version installed.

You can also determine the software version on your iPod touch by using iTunes. Connect the iPod touch to your computer and select it in the iTunes Source pane (in the Devices section). The iPod touch summary page appears to the right of the Source pane, and the software version appears next to the Software Version heading at the top of the page.

Updating with newer software

iTunes tells you whether your iPod touch has the newest software installed. Connect the iPod touch to your computer and select it in the iTunes Source pane (in the Devices section). The iPod touch Summary page appears to the right of the Source pane, as shown in Figure 14-2, and the Version section of the page tells you whether your iPod touch software is up-to-date and when iTunes will check for new software.

If an update is available, a dialog appears to ask permission to download it. Go ahead and click OK to update the iPod touch software; you'll be happy you did. After updating the software, iTunes continues syncing with the iPod touch until it is finished.

You can also check for new software at any time by clicking the Check for Update button on the Summary page.

Figure 14-2: Use iTunes to update or restore your iPod touch.

Restoring Your iPod touch

You can restore your iPod touch to its original factory condition. This operation erases its storage and returns the iPod touch to its original settings. If you intend to change the computer you're using for syncing your iPod touch, you have to restore the device, especially if you're switching from a Mac to a PC as your sync computer.

To replace content that was erased by the restore operation, sync your iPod touch from your computer's iTunes library, as I describe in Chapter 5.

Restoring previous settings

iTunes provides protection and backs up your iPod touch settings so that you can restore them. This backup comes in handy if you want to apply the settings to a new iPod touch or to an iPod touch that you had to restore to its factory conditions.

Whenever you synchronize your iPod touch, iTunes automatically copies all the settings you use to customize your iPod touch and its apps, including Wi-Fi network settings, the keyboard dictionary, and settings for contacts, calendars, and e-mail accounts.

To restore your settings, connect your new or restored iPod touch to the same computer and copy of iTunes you used before, so that iTunes remembers the backup settings. iTunes should open automatically. (If it doesn't, open iTunes manually.) Then follow the step-by-step instructions in Chapter 1 for connecting your iPod touch to iTunes and setting it up. As you continue through the setup screens, iTunes provides the option to restore the settings from a previously backed-up iPod touch or to set up the iPod touch as new. Choose the option to restore the settings and then click Continue to finish setting up your iPod touch.

To delete the backed-up settings for your iPod touch, open iTunes and choose iTunes⇨Preferences (on a Mac) or Edit⇨Preferences (on a Windows PC). Click the Devices tab, select the iPod touch in the Device Backups list, and then click Remove Backup. You don't need to connect your iPod touch to do this.

Restoring to factory conditions

Restoring an iPod touch erases its storage and sets all settings to their original default values. It's the last resort for fixing problems, and it's the only choice if you want to switch computers for syncing.

To restore an iPod touch, follow these steps for both the Mac and Windows versions of iTunes:

1. **Connect the iPod touch to your computer.**

   iTunes opens automatically.

2. **Select the iPod touch in the Devices section of the Source pane and click the Summary tab if it isn't already selected.**

   The iPod touch Summary pane appears to the right of the Source pane.

3. **Click the Restore button.**

   An alert dialog appears to confirm that you want to restore the iPod touch.

4. **Click the Restore button again to confirm the restore operation.**

   A progress bar appears, indicating the progress of the restore operation. iTunes notifies you when the restore is finished.

5. **Sync your iPod touch with content from your iTunes library.**

   Sync your iPod touch with the content in your library or manually manage your content, as I describe in Chapter 5.

6. **Sync your iPod touch with personal information (contacts, calendars, notes, e-mail accounts, and bookmarks).**

   Sync your iPod touch with your personal info, as I describe in Chapter 6.

7. **When you finish syncing, eject the iPod touch by clicking the Eject button next to its name in the Source pane.**

Now, with iPod touch restored, refreshed, and re-synced, you're ready to rock!

Part VI
The Part of Tens

The 5th Wave   By Rich Tennant

"Other than this little glitch with the landscape view, I really love my iPod touch."

*Y*ou've reached the last part, the part you've come to expect in every For Dummies book: This is the part that neatly encapsulates just about all the interesting aspects of this book's topic. Like the compilers of other important lists — David Letterman's Top Ten, the FBI's Ten Most Wanted, the Seven Steps to Heaven, the 12 Gates to the City, the 12 Steps to Recovery, The 13 Question Method, and the Billboard Hot 100 — I'm serious about the ritual of putting together the For Dummies Part of Tens.

And so, I offer in Chapter 15 ten tips not found elsewhere in the book, including keeping your battery juiced and your screen clean; rating your songs, deleting apps, videos, and podcasts from your iPod touch; and using international keyboards for different languages, including handwritten Chinese.

In Chapter 16, the last chapter of this book, I've compiled ten great apps for the iPod touch that shook the iPod world and changed it forever. These consist of the apps not mentioned elsewhere in this book that you can obtain from the App Store — many of them free.

15

Ten Tangible Tips

*T*his book is filled with tips, but I've put in this chapter ten truly handy ones that didn't fit in elsewhere but which can help make your iPod touch experience a completely satisfying one.

Saving the Life of Your Battery

Follow these simple rules:

✓ Don't keep an iPod touch in a snug carrying case when charging — that snug case can cause overheating.

✓ Top it off with power whenever it's convenient.

✓ Set your iPod touch to automatically go to sleep by choosing Settings⇨General⇨ Auto-Lock from the Home screen.

Everything else you need to know is in Chapter 1.

Keeping Your Screen Clean

If the iPod touch display has excessive moisture on it from humidity or wet fingers, wipe it with a soft, dry cloth. If it's dirty, use a soft, slightly damp, lint-free cloth — an inexpensive eyeglass cleaning cloth sold in vision care stores or pharmacies is a good choice. By no means should you use window cleaners, household cleaners, aerosol sprays, solvents, alcohol, ammonia, or abrasives — they can scratch or otherwise damage the display. Also, try not to get any moisture in any of the openings, as it could short out the device.

Getting Healthy with Nike

Use your iPod touch as a workout companion with Nike+ running shoes and a Nike+ iPod Sport Kit. Its sensor fits inside your Nike+ shoe under the insole. The current-generation iPod touch includes a receiver, but the first-generation iPod touch requires a separate receiver.

When you have the kit and the shoes, activate the app on your iPod touch — choose Settings➪Nike + iPod and tap Off for the Nike + iPod option to turn it on. You can track your pace, time, and distance from one workout to the next, and you can pick songs and playlists to match. You can even sync your workout data with nikeplus.com, see all your runs, and share motivation with runners across the world.

Rating Your Songs

Ratings are useful — the Shuffle and Genius features are influenced by ratings, and you can define smart playlists with ratings to select only rated songs so you can avoid the clunkers and spinal tappers. In fact, when you try to put a music library on your iPod touch that's larger than the device's capacity, iTunes decides which songs to synchronize based on — you guessed it, *ratings*.

iTunes lets you rate your songs, but so does your iPod touch. You can rate any song on your iPod touch as you listen to it. Ratings you assign on your iPod touch are automatically resynchronized back to your iTunes library when you connect your iPod touch again.

To assign a rating to a song on your iPod touch, follow these steps:

1. **Start playing a song (see Chapter 7 for details).**

   The Now Playing screen appears.

2. **Tap the List button to display a list of the album or playlist contents.**

   The List button is in the upper-right corner.

3. **Tap the title of any song in the track listing or leave selected the song that's playing.**

4. **Drag across the ratings bar at the top of the track listing to give the song zero to five stars.**

   The upper limit is five stars (for the best).

Deleting Apps from Your iPod touch

You can turn off the synchronization of certain apps in your iTunes library before syncing your iPod touch to iTunes, as I describe in Chapter 5, so that the apps disappear from your iPod touch. But you can also delete apps directly from your iPod touch.

Touch and hold any icon on the Home screen until all the icons begin to wiggle (as if you're about to rearrange them or add Home screens). To delete an app, tap the circled *X* that appears inside the app's icon as it wiggles. Your iPod touch displays a warning that deleting the app also deletes all its data; tap Delete to go ahead and delete the app and its data or tap Cancel to cancel.

To stop the icons from wiggling, press the Home button on the device, which saves any changes you made to your Home screens.

Deleting Videos and Podcasts from Your iPod touch

Need more room on your iPod touch? You can delete a video or podcast episode directly from your iPod touch by flicking left or right across the video or podcast episode selection and then tapping the Delete button that appears, as shown in Figure 15-1.

Your video or podcast episode is deleted from your iPod touch only. When you sync your iPod touch with iTunes, the video or podcast episode is copied back to your iPod touch. If you want to prevent the video or podcast episode from appearing on your iPod touch after syncing, deselect it first before syncing your iPod touch, or switch to manually managing music and videos, as I describe in Chapter 5. *Note:* If you delete a rented movie from an iPod touch, it's gone forever (or until you rent it again).

Measuring Traffic in Maps

The Maps app not only shows you the route to take, but in some areas it can also show you traffic patterns so you can avoid the jams. The traffic data is constantly updated and aggregated from a variety of Internet sources by Google. It is available for more than 30 major U.S. cities, including New York, Los Angeles, San Francisco, and Washington.

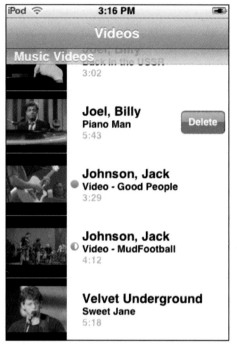

Figure 15-1: Flick left or right across the video or podcast episode to see the Delete button.

To use Maps, tap the Maps icon on the Home screen. The Maps app appears (refer to Chapter 12). You can obtain directions first, as I describe in Chapter 12, or just display any location on the map that has highways. To show traffic information, tap the Underneath button (the curled page icon in the bottom-right corner) to see a menu underneath the map and then tap Show Traffic.

When the map shows traffic, highways are color-coded according to the flow of traffic:

- Green for highways moving faster than 50 miles per hour (mph)
- Yellow for 25–50 mph
- Red for less than 25 mph

If you don't see color-coded highways, you may need to zoom out to see high-ways and major roads.

To stop showing the traffic, tap the Underneath button and then tap Hide Traffic.

Turning On International Keyboards

You can turn on keyboards for different languages and use them simultaneously. To turn on international keyboards, choose Settings⇨General⇨Keyboard from the Home screen and then tap International Keyboards (scroll the list to find it). The international keyboards appear, as shown in Figure 15-2.

You can turn on any of the keyboards you need — tap Off to turn each one on. To access languages with more than one keyboard, such as Japanese, tap Japanese first and then tap the specific keyboard layout (QWERTY or Kana).

You can then switch keyboards while typing information by tapping the globe icon, as shown in Figure 15-3, that appears to the right of the .?123 key when more than one international keyboard is turned on. The language of the newly active keyboard appears briefly in the spacebar.

iPod 🛜	2:06 PM	🔋
◀ Keyboard	**Keyboards**	
English		ON
English (UK)		OFF
Arabic		OFF
Bulgarian		OFF
Czech		OFF
Danish		OFF
German		ON
Greek		OFF
Spanish		ON

Figure 15-2: Turn on international keyboards.

Each time you tap the globe icon, the keyboard layout switches to the next language you've turned on, in the order that they appear in the international keyboards list.

For example, if you turned on English, English (UK), German, and Japanese Kana (for a total of 4 keyboards), tapping the globe icon switches from English to English (UK). Tapping it again switches to German, and tapping it again switches to Japanese Kana. Tapping the globe icon one more time switches back to English.

To use the Japanese Kana keyboard, use the keypad to select syllables. For more syllable options, tap the arrow key and select another syllable or word from the window. With the Japanese QWERTY keyboard, you can use the QWERTY layout to input code for Japanese syllables. As you type, suggested syllables appear, and you can tap the syllable to choose it.

Figure 15-3: Switch to another language.

Drawing Chinese Characters

The iPod touch offers keyboards for both Traditional and Simplified Chinese, with Handwriting and Pinyin layouts for both. Turn on international keyboards as described in the preceding section and tap Chinese (Simplified) or Chinese (Traditional). Then tap Off to turn on Handwriting or Pinyin. (You can turn both on.)

For the Handwriting layouts, use the touchpad to enter Chinese characters with your finger, as shown in Figure 15-4.

As you draw character strokes, matching characters appear in a list, with the closest match at the top. When you choose a character, its related characters appear in the list as additional choices.

For Simplified Pinyin, use the QWERTY keyboard to enter Pinyin for Chinese characters; as you type, suggested Chinese characters appear. Tap a character to choose it or continue entering Pinyin to see more character options.

Figure 15-4: Drawing Chinese characters.

Stopping a Wi-Fi Network From Joining

Your iPod touch remembers your Wi-Fi connections and automatically uses one when it detects it within your range. If you've used multiple Wi-Fi networks in the same location, it picks the last one you used. (For details on choosing a Wi-Fi network, see Chapter 4.)

But if your iPod touch keeps picking up a Wi-Fi network that you can't properly join, such as a private network that requires a password you don't know or a commercial network that charges for access, you can tell your iPod touch to *forget* this particular network, rather than turning off Wi-Fi itself. This is very useful if a paid service has somehow gotten hold of your iPod touch and won't let you move on to other Web pages without typing a password.

Choose Settings⇨Wi-Fi from the Home screen and tap the circled right-arrow (>) button next to the selected network's name. The network's information screen appears. Tap the Forget This Network button at the top of the screen so that your iPod touch doesn't join it automatically. Then tap the Wi-Fi Networks button at the top-left corner to return to the Wi-Fi Networks screen. You can always select this network manually, and you can still continue to use other Wi-Fi networks.

Ten Apps That Shook the iPod World

In This Chapter

▶ Apps that show how an iPod touch can control your world

▶ Apps that demonstrate the iPod touch experience to the hilt

▶ Apps I use all the time that aren't mentioned elsewhere in this book

*1*t's not fair. Only ten apps? As I write this, over 50,000 apps from almost as many software companies are competing for attention in the App Store. I could write an entire book about just the ones that have shaken *my* world — right down to the very routines I live by. (Maybe they'll let me write that book in the future.) Instead, the publisher dragged me kicking and screaming to the back of the book, and told me we'd run out of room and that we had to keep it to ten.

How did I pick these ten? I included apps I think are important as an introduction to the iPod touch ex-perience, along with the apps that I use every day.

I left out of this list the ones I've already described in other chapters and on the Cheat Sheet of this book — Facebook, MySpace, Twitterific, Skype, and the messaging apps (Chapter 13); Google Earth (Chapter 12); Wikipanion and other wiki readers (Chapter 10); Pandora, Truveo, and other apps that stream video (Chapter 8); PocketGuitar and other apps that help you make music (Chapter 7); a variety of games that use time (Chapter 3) or the accelerometer (Chapter 2); and the apps for fun and travel (Cheat Sheet). I also left out, of course, Apple's apps that are supplied with the iPod touch. And yet, all of these apps, and especially the ones from Apple, are responsible for shak-ing up the iPod world.

Remote

The Remote app from Apple (free) turns your iPod touch into a remote control for iTunes and Apple TV. It was the first app to demonstrate how the iPod touch could be transformed by software into a completely different functional handheld device. The Remote app works with your Wi-Fi network, so you can control playback from anywhere in and around your home.

Enigmo

Voted the best game at the 2008 Worldwide Developers Conference and winner of various awards, Enigmo (not free) is a unique 3D puzzle game in which you direct animated flowing streams of water, oil, and lava, using your iPod touch to move and rotate the various puzzle pieces in order to divert the flow of the falling droplets so that they can reach their target.

Tap Tap Revenge

With a name obviously inspired by Japan's megapopular Dance Dance Revolution, the original Tap Tap Revenge (free) takes its cues from the addictive Guitar Hero, putting your rhythmic skills to the test. You tap through the beats of the music or shake left and right as the arrows fall. Tap Tap Revenge 2, also free, offers more than 150 free tracks to download as well as an immersive 3D experience.

Flick Fishing

Okay all you old-timers, bait those hooks! Flick Fishing's animated environment all but puts the "Gone fishing" sign on your office door. Flick Fishing (not free) lets you cast a line with just a flick of your wrist and reel it in, but you have to be careful to avoid snapping the "line" and losing the "fish." Of course, larger fish are stronger and not so easily reeled in.

Ocarina

By far the most famous of strange new iPhone apps that defy characterization, Ocarina (not free) — the app that turns your iPhone into an ancient, flute-like instrument and lets you share the music you make with others —

now works with the iPod touch as well. Without any musical training, you can touch the holes of the ocarina to make music or blow into an external microphone.

iBeer

It would be remiss of me to not include the best of the sight gag (and sound gag) apps. Although I'm not a fan of embarrassing noises, I do like visual gags, and iBeer (not free) has taken the lead in downloads. Your iPod touch behaves, well, like a glass of beer. It takes full advantage of the accelerometer so that you can tilt to sip from it, shake for more foam, and even pour beer from one iPod touch to another.

Google Mobile

Searching with Google has always been part of Safari (see Chapter 10). Google Mobile (free) provides instant access to Google Search, Gmail, Google News, Docs, Calendar, Talk, and other Google apps. You get relevant search suggestions as you type, and you can use location search to find businesses, services, weather, and movie info, and then see these suggestions on Google Maps.

Mobile News

Don't like the news you read in the papers? Rather than going out and making some of your own, try The AP Mobile News Network app (free) — powered by the Associated Press — which offers access to local and national news from trusted sources. AP is typically the source for many newspaper articles. I read all my news on my iPod touch: It's free, it saves paper, and it's updated more frequently.

Stanza

The Stanza app (free) changed my reading habits — I not only read more classics (which are mostly free), but I also read everywhere I go. You can download a vast selection of over 50,000 free classics and over 50,000 contemporary works and read them right on your iPod touch. Sort by title or author or create custom collections to build reading lists and keep track of all your books. Although other readers have appeared (notably the Amazon Kindle Reader and eReader), Stanza is my favorite.

Tony's Tips

Tony's Tips for iPhone Users Manual (not free), developed and published by yours truly, is an app that provides helpful tips for using your iPhone or iPod touch with iTunes and MobileMe. I add new tips and revise the information regularly as Apple updates the software — the information is online, and the app that connects to it lets you search for and read topics and save pages for offline reading.

Index